Haviland China
The Age of Elegance

Nora Travis

Revised Price Guide

4880 Lower Valley Rd. Atglen, PA 19310 USA

Library of Congress Cataloging-in-Publication Data

Travis, Nora.
    Haviland china: the age of elegance/Nora Travis.
        p.   cm.
    Includes bibliographical references and index.
    ISBN: 0-7643-0490-9   (hardcover)
    1. Haviland china--Collectors and collecting--
Catalogs. I. Title.
    NK4399.H4T73   1997
    738.2'0944'66--dc20   96-27168
                                                        CIP

Published by Schiffer Publishing Ltd.
4880 Lower Valley Road
Atglen, PA 19310
Phone: (610) 593-1777; Fax: (610) 593-2002
E-mail: schifferbk@aol.com
Please write for a free catalog.
This book may be purchased from the publisher.
Please include $3.95 for shipping.
Try your bookstore first.

We are interested in hearing from authors
with book ideas on related subjects.

Price Guide

Revised price guide: 1998
Copyright © 1997 by Nora Travis

Printed in China

ISBN: 0-7643-0490-9

The prices for the Haviland pieces shown in this book have been listed in a range from low to high. Prices vary from region to region, seller to seller and condition of the item. In dinnerware, some patterns are more in demand than others and, therefore, command a higher price. In regard to unusual pieces, prices can fluctuate even more, depending on how rare the item is.

I have tried to get as close to the actual prices as possible, but again, this is a guide and all of the above must be taken into consideration. Neither the author nor the publisher assumes any responsibility for any losses that a collector may incur while using this guide.

Contents

Acknowledgments

Since 1989, Haviland China has been a very large part of my life and I am pleased to be able to share some of the things that I have learned during these last few years. This book might not have been written except for the encouragement of my daughter, Patricia Anders, who also edited the text for me.

David Reichard, who passed away in December 1995, was very helpful in giving me little tips about the Haviland china replacement business in the early years when I was a novice. "Haviland Dave," as he was known around town, had such a great knowledge of Haviland china and he will be missed.

Rick Zimring at Kits Cameras was an enormous help in teaching me the fundamentals and fine art of porcelain photography. He tutored me through roll after roll of mistakes until I was able to produce the crisp and clear photos shown in this book. He also personally developed each roll to assure their perfect color.

Special thanks to Marty Tackitt and Roger and Julie Mairs for allowing me to photograph their extensive and unusual collections. They have helped make this book a work of art. Also a thank you to Art Wendt for sending me negatives of special Haviland pieces in his collection for inclusion in this book.

A special note of thanks to the Board of the Haviland Collectors Internationale Foundation for the loan of special negatives, plus all of their encouragement and support.

A very special thank you to Dr. W.J. Tomasini, retired professor of Art History at the University of Iowa, who so graciously took on the job of proofreading and editing my text for historical accuracy. His suggestions have made this a better book. Dr. Tomasini has been a collector of Haviland china for many years and has done extensive research on dining with Haviland. He is the author of *Celebrating 150 years of Haviland China*, published by the Haviland Collectors Internationale Foundation (HCIF) for the special museum display at the Villa Terrace Decorative Arts Museum in Milwaukee, Wisconsin, in 1992.

Last, but not least, I want to thank the rest of my family: my husband, Donald, for his many hours of patience as I took over every inch of space in the house with Haviland china or research materials, and his love and support in all my endeavors; my daughter, Lori, who listened to me moan about not having enough time to work on this book; my parents who gave me a love for beautiful things and enthusiastically encouraged me to write this book; my father-in-law for suggesting that I contact his cousin, Mildred; and all of my friends and customers who spurred me on by asking, "Is it almost finished?"

Foreword

This copiously illustrated general survey of the history of the production of Haviland dinnerware is an important addition to both the literature on general porcelain production and tableware and also American cultural history. As a collector and one of the founders and past presidents of the Haviland Collectors Internationale Foundation (HCIF) and the Haviland Collectors Internationale Educational Foundation (HCIEF), I appreciate this significant contribution made by Nora Travis. For the first time the public has the opportunity to connect and relate the multiplicity of sizes, types, shapes, and functions of plates, cups and serving pieces with the changing customs and etiquette of the American dining table. Ms. Travis thereby places Haviland dinnerware in the context of American cultural history and society for the past one hundred and fifty years.

Both possessors of Haviland and the vast public of collectors and dealers of other types of dinnerware can now be informed of the significant role played by the Haviland family and its porcelain production. In the areas of technology, production, aesthetics, design innovation, and international marketing practice, Haviland led the way and helped change forever American attitudes about the dining table, dining, and dining etiquette. Porcelain and ceramic pieces produced by this American entrepreneurial family can be honored and remembered for adapting the best quality of French Limoges porcelain to the taste and table of a broad range of the American public from presidents and tycoons to the solid middle class. This American and French commercial, industrial and cultural alliance is a story worth telling, and a story worth reading.

W.J.Tomasini, Ph.D.
Professor, History of Art
University of Iowa

Preface

Over the past 150 years, people have treasured Haviland china, handing it down generation after generation. Haviland collectors often ask me about those who created such fragile yet enduring dinnerware and about those who used it to grace their tables. The purpose of this book is to answer those questions and to show through photographs the beauty that is Haviland china.

With the inception of the Haviland Collectors Internationale Foundation in 1989, dealers and collectors throughout the United States and Europe have gathered with one purpose: furthering the knowledge of Haviland china. Over the last few years, this organization has located original old catalogs and documents, enabling collectors and dealers to have valuable information regarding all aspects of Haviland china.

This book will attempt to give a brief history of the Haviland family, plus a history of dining throughout the span of Haviland china, including research of old cookery books that gave style, recipes and menus for the mid- to late 1800s. As food tastes changed through the decades, the usage of various pieces of china also changed. In studying the dining habits over the last century, we can learn about the various pieces of dinnerware and how they were used. The reader must keep this in mind as I have shown pieces listed as one thing which ten years later might have been used for something else.

With the years of usage, pieces have acquired certain names as they were handed down in the family.

Grandmother might have used her open oval vegetable bowl for mashed potatoes; therefore, it was called the "mashed potato bowl." I have attached the correct names to many pieces by researching the old catalogs. Depending on the year of the catalog, the names might have changed, but I have tried to be as accurate as I can. As many different patterns as possible have been photographed, enabling you to identify your Haviland pattern. There are still many more patterns and types of pieces that could be identified, but there had to be a stopping point. Perhaps I will be able to cover additional patterns in the future, if there is a next book!

This book also includes some information on the china of Charles Field Haviland, Theodore Haviland *Made in America*, Johann Haviland, and some examples of the more recent productions of Haviland & Company — only because I hope this book can provide answers to your questions. I hope the collector, as well as the "inheritor," will find something of interest and enjoyment.

For more detailed information, I recommend that you purchase *CELEBRATING 150 YEARS OF HAVILAND CHINA 1842-1992* from the Haviland Collectors Internationale Foundation, P. O. Box 11632, Milwaukee, WI 53211.

If you have any questions regarding Haviland china, you may contact me by writing to P.O. Box 6008, Suite 161, Cerritos, CA 90701 or by telephone, (714) 521-9283. Please include a self-addressed stamped envelope.

Genealogy of the Havilands

THE HAVILANDS *
A Family of Porcelain Makers

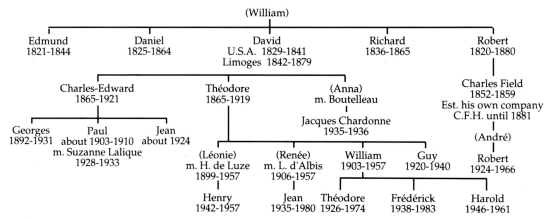

(William)

Edmund	Daniel	David	Richard	Robert
1821-1844	1825-1864	U.S.A. 1829-1841	1836-1865	1820-1880
		Limoges 1842-1879		

Charles-Edward 1865-1921 · Théodore 1865-1919 · (Anna) m. Boutelleau

Charles Field 1852-1859 Est. his own company C.F.H. until 1881

Jacques Chardonne 1935-1936

(André)

Georges 1892-1931 · Paul about 1903-1910 m. Suzanne Lalique 1928-1933 · Jean about 1924

(Léonie) m. H. de Luze 1899-1957 · (Renée) m. L. d'Albis 1906-1957 · William 1903-1957 · Guy 1920-1940 · Robert 1924-1966

Henry 1942-1957 · Jean 1935-1980 · Théodore 1926-1974 · Frédérick 1938-1983 · Harold 1946-1961

* The dates indicate an individual's participation in the business.
The names in parentheses were not involved in the business.

Taken from J. d'Albis, <u>Haviland</u>, p. 8

Part 1:
The Beginning of Haviland China

David Haviland Creates a Legacy

David Haviland (1814-1879) was one of eight brothers, seven of whom worked in the tableware trade. Edmond, the oldest, purchased a tableware shop from his employer in 1821 and primarily sold English creamware and Staffordshire in his shop in New York City. In 1829, Edmund brought David, age 15, into the shop as an apprentice and later made him a partner.

Economic marketing failures of the late 1830s seriously affected English imports, prompting David to open his own tableware import company with his brother Daniel in 1838, with the idea of expanding into French porcelain. They called their company the "D.G. and D. Haviland Company," until 1852 when brother Robert came into the company, changing the name to "Haviland Brothers & Company."

In 1840, David made his first trip to France to establish an alliance with a manufacturer who could design and create pieces of porcelain dinnerware for his company. David realized that to assure himself of the quality of the Haviland china being shipped to New York, someone from the family would need to reside in France. Therefore, in the Autumn of 1841, David sailed with his wife Mary, and their first son Charles Edward (1839-1921), to Foecy in the province of Berry to stay with friends, the Pilluvyt family. They, like the Havilands, were Quakers as well as china-makers. The Haviland family eventually settled in Limoges in April of 1842, and in September, their second son Theodore (1842-1919) was born.

From 1842 to 1847, to satisfy his customers overseas, David created molds which would adapt the shapes of the china to American tastes. He had the local factories make the pieces, commissioned local artisans to decorate them and then shipped the porcelain to the family store in New York. In 1847, David was able to open his own decoration workshop.

In September of 1853, the French government granted David permission to build his own porcelain factory, and by May 1855, he had the muffle kilns and decoration workshops in full operation. David was very busy during these formative years: winning the gold medal at the New York Crystal Palace Exhibition in 1853 and the silver medal at the Paris Exhibition in 1855. He was constantly creating new designs and new methods of decoration, introducing American factory methods into the production of the porcelain. David was instrumental in uniting the production of whiteware with the decorating process, which in turn produced major changes in the manufacturing process of porcelain in Limoges. Watching the success of the Haviland Company inspired the French and European companies to compete for a portion of the American and international trade.

At that time, France was considered to be the center of cultural and decorative arts. Napoleon III and his wife, the Empress Eugenie, were on the throne setting standards in style and taste which were copied throughout the world. Consequently, porcelain manufactured by the Haviland Brothers & Company grew to be a highly successful and sought-after commodity.

The North's Naval Blockade of the South during the American Civil War brought about a serious decline in imports, enough that the company was not able to survive. Since many of their customers were in the southern states, Haviland Brothers & Company was forced to close its doors in 1863. The facility in France had been only a subsidiary of the New York firm and when that business had to close, David Haviland saw this as an opportunity to open his own porcelain manufacturing company in Limoges, France named Haviland & Company.

David set about constructing the large kilns to fire the porcelain whiteware, and in 1865, as soon as production was ready to begin, he brought his two sons, Charles Edward, age 25, and Theodore, age 23, into the business. Charles Edward was very astute at managing and took over increased responsibilities, while Theodore excelled at marketing and sales. At the end of the Civil War, David sent Theodore to America to handle the distribution and marketing of the china, especially in the northern states. Within a year or two of opening Haviland & Company, David had completely turned over the management to Charles Edward. David Haviland died in 1879, secure in the knowledge that he had launched a company that would become a household word throughout the world.

Charles Edward Haviland and the Industrial Revolution

Brilliant and strong willed, Charles Edward was always looking for ways to create better designs and faster production. A French engineer, Francois Faure, designed a plate-calibrating machine that would revolutionize the ceramics industry; a machine which in some instances is still in use today. Charles Edward was one of the first to purchase this machine for his factory, marking the beginning of mechanization in this industry.

Production dramatically increased during the years after the American Civil War and with Haviland china becoming an international product, we can appreciate the organization it must have taken to run such a company. Limoges was a provincial town during the late 1860s and early 1870s; transportation and communication were both limited. Charles Edward, who gave great attention to detail, had his finger on every aspect of production, from the artists' renderings and creation of the pieces to the orders and shipments of the final products.

Like his father before him, Charles Edward sought the most talented artists to design the molds and artwork. In 1872, Charles Edward met Felix Bracquemond, head of the painter's workshop at the Sevres factory. As Haviland & Company was in the process of developing a design studio in Paris, the Auteuil Studio, Charles Edward thought that Bracquemond would be the most qualified to head the facility. During this time, Bracquemond was with Haviland and he was responsible for many innovative ideas (see Decorative Ware). He signed a ten-year contract, but because of creative differences with Charles Edward, Bracquemond stayed for only nine years. In a quote from Jean d'Albis' book on Haviland, Charles Edward clearly established responsibilities from the start: *"I intend to give you absolute freedom in all artistic matters, but it is absolutely essential that I approve all commercial samples. I must be convinced I can sell them and, in this matter, I am not ready to accept anyone else's judgement when it does not coincide with mine."* (Oct. 7th, 1872). Charles Edward assumed complete control of the Auteuil Studio, but continued to employ only the most gifted of artists such as Pallandre, Lindeneher and the Dammouse brothers.

In 1867, David had written a contract between himself and his two sons in which David kept two-fifths of the shares of the factory, Charles Edward two-fifths and Theodore only one-fifth. When Theodore Haviland returned to Limoges in 1879 upon the death of his father, he took charge of manufacturing. Charles Edward and Theodore had been at odds for years, and working in such close proximity brought their relationship to an end. Theodore wanted to have equal say in all matters, but Charles Edward would not let him. Charles Edward kept a tight rein on the family in every aspect of their lives. The brothers knew they had to separate and so, on December 31st, 1891, Haviland & Company closed its doors. It opened the following day under the same name with Charles Edward and his eldest son Georges running the new operation.

Realizing what a despot he was, Charles Edward knew that Theodore would never be happy under his direction. When Theodore purchased a piece of land to build his own workshops, the Theodore Haviland Company, there was no animosity between them.

Charles Edward married a middle-class French girl who died at the age of 30 in 1873. Four years later, at age 38, he married Helene, a young girl of 17 who came from an important Parisian family. Charles Edward learned quite a lot regarding artistic creation from her father, Philippe Burty, a well-known art critic. Charles Edward had three sons: Georges, Paul and Jean. He brought Georges into the business in 1892; and in 1921, upon the death of his father, Georges assumed leadership of the company.

In 1926 a large fire destroyed many of the warehouses and the designing room of Haviland & Company. Many of the patterns and records were lost for all time, and in September of 1929, just a month before the Crash on Wall Street, another great fire devoured the contents of the Haviland museum as well as other warehouses. With the Great Depression of 1929, sales in America slowed to a trickle until production was completely stopped in 1930, forcing Haviland & Company to liquidate its assets in 1931.

Theodore Haviland

Theodore Haviland was born in France in 1842, but spent so many years in the United States that he felt himself to be American — unlike his brother Charles Edward, who had been born in the United States, but felt very French as he spent the majority of his life in France. At the age of 23, Theodore sailed to America to become the factory representative for Haviland & Company.

He was as creative as both his father and his brother; during his stay in America, he used his creativity to market Haviland china. He hoped to convince every household in America that they couldn't live without this special dinnerware and tried several marketing strategies to further his goal.

During summer, when sales were slack, he traveled back to France. He would spend the time in Limoges meeting the factory workers, maintaining contact with the foremen with whom he had to work, discussing new ideas and plans with David and Charles Edward, and showing them earthenware samples from other competitors that he brought back with him.

Sample products presented a difficult problem in those days as they were very heavy and difficult to carry. Sample books were hand-painted at first, then when photography was available in 1878, things became a little easier. Theodore assembled a book of photographs for each salesman, showing the different versions of the sample piece they carried. The books were bound in the States and, as new pieces were created, the pages were sent to America to be added.

Figure 1. Round covered vegetable, salesman's sample with several different patterns. Has stock and tariff numbers on bottom with backstamps. Haviland & Company, 1888-1896, Marks H and c (The Marks in this and all other photographs refer to the Haviland Blank and Decorator Marks listed in the back of the book and are listed alphabetically in upper and lower case as shown.). $125-175.

Figure 2. Fish plate, salesman's sample. Cobalt and gold trim on
Marseille blank. Haviland & Company, 1876-1889, Marks F and c.
Courtesy of Marty Tackitt. $125-225.

Figure 3. Back of fish plate, salesman's sample, shows stock
number, name of the blank and price.

Autumn and spring were the busiest seasons for Theodore. He would sail back to the United States and resume his travels from one end of the country to the other. Since the building of the Union Pacific Railroad in 1859, travel from coast-to-coast was easier and faster; and by 1865, Theodore was able to expand his territories across to the Pacific. Trade boomed in 1866 and the factory couldn't keep up with all of the orders!

Theodore lived on East 30th Street in New York City, within easy walking distance of the shop on 45 Barker Street. He worked in the New York office from 1864 to 1866 with the assistance of his cousins, the Willards. As sales grew, he added more staff.

Theodore spent a great deal of time with U.S. Customs as every tenth cask had to be opened and inspected. Breakage, unfortunately, was high. The porcelain was placed in wooden casks, packed with wet hay and strapped with split sapling hoops. These casks could hold more than twenty cubic feet and if the china was not packed correctly, it would break in shipment. The workers had to be trained to pack correctly to keep breakage at a minimum. However, with army recruitment laws in France requiring all able bodied men to serve in the military, and workers having to be replaced frequently to serve their tours of duty, training was not very thorough. By using casks, dock workers could roll them onto the ship and tie them into the hold so they could not move. However, the wooden stays would come loose and china would still break.

Charles Edward has been given most of the credit for the modernization of porcelain making, but Theodore was also innovative in many ways. Marketing of the product was very important, and he succeeded in building up the American trade so much that Haviland was forced to give up some of the market to other manufacturers as they couldn't keep up with the demand for quality china.

Both Theodore and Charles Edward were disturbed about American porcelain manufacturers and other companies copying their designs. They had to farm out molds and porcelain for other Limoges companies to fire to keep up with the enormous quantity of orders they needed to fill, and they were concerned with maintaining both the quality of Haviland china and their company's good name. At that time, it was not required to stamp every piece for import and so Haviland was able to fill orders with unsigned porcelain made to their specifications.

It was Theodore who suggested that Haviland stamp their name on all pieces they manufactured themselves to protect their reputation. In 1876, Theodore encouraged Haviland & Company to put their customers' shop names on the bottom of each piece as a form of advertising to entice the china shops to buy Haviland products. Therefore, when we see a plate with *S.A.Boyd, San Diego* or *Gumps, San Francisco* included in the back mark, it shows that the piece was sold by that particular china shop.

By 1886, there were approximately 120 retailers selling Haviland china in the United States, and the number was increasing all the time. Because Theodore was there in the United States with the customer, he had to handle all of the complaints that came to Haviland & Company. Customers objected that some of the colors washed off, or they wanted better quality; but the main grievance was that it took too long for their china to be delivered — an average of four months by ship. Theodore was able to convince Charles Edward to reduce this time to ninety days.

Theodore met his future wife, Julie, on an ocean liner on one of his crossings to France in 1873. The following year, they were married in Paris at the American Embassy. They moved to a residence on Lexington Avenue in New York City, and Theodore went back to selling Haviland until 1879. David being very ill, Theodore and Julie packed up and moved back to France. As previously stated, Theodore and Charles did not always agree on the way to run the company and there was a lot of dissension between the brothers.

A New Company is Created

Theodore Haviland purchased a twelve-acre plot of land, which is now located on the Place David Haviland in Limoges. He secured exclusive contracts with William Briggs, the New York agent for Haviland & Company, enabling him to keep sales flowing to America. On August 3, 1893, Theodore's factory, the Theodore Haviland Company, was formally inaugurated. At that time, it was considered to be the most modern in Limoges with electric lithograph presses that could do four times more work than the steam-driven presses used in other factories.

Many artists, who had formerly been connected with Haviland & Company were called upon to design for Theodore Haviland. Theodore became known for his more elaborate designs and table decorations, and had a fondness for porcelain blanks with designs molded into the surfaces. A new paste composition was developed, "porcelaine mousseline," which allowed for a whiter and thinner ware.

The Theodore Haviland Company was honored with the highest award, "The Grand Prix," at the 1900 Paris Exposition Universelle. Five molded figure busts by sculptor Bourdelle and a celadon and white table service designed by Dammouse for Queen Maria Pia of Portugal were among the items that were submitted at this exposition and were judged excellent in quality and originality.

His eldest son, William, joined the company in 1903 and became a director in 1904. There were unending problems with the Customs Office in America as 28,450 barrels of china were imported in 1906, compared with the 753 barrels listed in 1842. The American Potters Association forced U.S. Customs to impose a ban on imports from February to June of 1907, creating a large layoff of people and reducing sales dramatically in the American market. This embargo forced a "Rate List" to be created, a new tariff based on the average selling price of porcelain in Limoges.

From 1914 to 1917 was a difficult time for the Haviland Companies. World War I brought shortages of coal, plaster and lack of workmen, as well as problems with exporting. However, contrary to rumors, neither of the Haviland factories were ever bombed during either world war. China firings, which numbered 205 in 1914, fell to only 51 in 1917.

Change of an Era

Upon the death of Theodore Haviland on December 17, 1919, William, Theodore's eldest son, became Chairman of the Board. It remained a family business as Guy Haviland, William's brother, and H. de Luze and L. d'Albis, his two brothers-in-law, helped him in the operation of the company.

After World War I, there was a big change in the way people lived — things were much simpler. People didn't want to waste time sitting at the dinner table eating enormous meals. They wanted to get out and *"live it up,"* and the birth of the Contemporary Era brought about a great change in design for the porcelain business. Place settings were limited in quantity of pieces, and serving pieces were just the basic. Gone were the individual butter dishes, bone dishes and other special pieces that would have been used in the many-course dinners of the past. Also, the introduction of colored pastes and the near disappearance of decoration gave a completely different look to the china.

By 1921, William became conscious of the new trends and was able to show the earlier designed Sandoz and the later Dufy etc., at the *l'Exposition des Arts Decoratifs* in 1925. He visited the exposition with Dufy which further entrenched him in the new styles. William was so convinced that the public would only be interested in his new innovative designs that he did not hesitate to destroy many of the old molds to make room for the new designs. Laforet, the old mold maker, wrote with regret in his registry that the old models he had carved 30 years before with such love were no more.

The Great Depression of 1929 almost destroyed the Limoges porcelain industry. German, Czech and French dinnerware flooded the market as tons of porcelain was sold at giveaway prices by companies forced into bankruptcy. Theodore Haviland Company was very heavily affected as 70 percent of their production was shipped to the United States. Sales of Haviland china dropped dramatically until 1944, when they leveled off and started climbing back somewhat; but production never again ran as high as before.

In 1936, to increase the market for dinnerware, William Haviland formed a porcelain factory in America, which operated in New Castle, Pennsylvania until 1957. The American Haviland, labeled *Theodore Haviland, Made in America*, became a success during that time with beautiful and basic designs. Since Limoges and other areas of France were under Nazi occupation, Haviland was not able to transport the Limoges kaolin to America. They were forced to use kaolin found in local regions, but this clay was not as pure as that found in Limoges; therefore, the American Haviland china was of a heavier weight, and did not have the translucent whiteness of the porcelain made in Limoges. It was also of a softer paste and could scratch easily.

With the simplification of design and shape, William Haviland gave new life to the porcelain industry. Because the simple patterns were more cost efficient, the factory was able to weather the Depression and World War II. In 1941, William and his brothers-in-law were able to buy all of the designs, trademarks and rights of the original Haviland & Company created by David Haviland a century before and Haviland Société Anonyme was formed, bringing both companies back under one name. When William retired in 1957, his son Harold took over management. In 1961, Theodore, William's other son, became president and Theodore's son Frederick became the manager of the New York office.

Figure 4. Salad plate, *Rosalinde.* Theodore Haviland, Made in America, 1936-1957, Mark T. $20-35.

The Haviland family retired from management of the company in 1972 and it is currently owned by Mr. Dominique de Coster, who restructured the company in 1992, moving the decorating plant from the middle of Limoges to join with the whiteware plant housed in a modern industrial park on the outskirts of town.

Figure 5. Tea cup and saucer, *Apple Blossom.* Theodore Haviland, Made in America, 1936-1957, Mark T. $32-50.

Charles Field Haviland and Robert Haviland

In 1852, David Haviland's 20-year-old nephew, Charles Field Haviland, sailed to France to begin an apprenticeship with his Uncle David in importing and exporting procedures. In 1858, Charles Field married Marie Louise Mallevergne. Her grandfather, Francois Alluaud, had established a whiteware factory, Casseaux Works, in 1797; within a year of his marriage, Charles Field set himself up in business as a decorator of porcelain produced by Casseaux Works.

Francois Alluaud's two sons ran the Casseaux Works until their deaths, both in 1876; since Charles Field was the sole surviving male in the family and women at that time were not allowed to engage in business, he took over management of the factory. Charles Field copied his Uncle David's methods of combining whiteware and decoration under one roof.

In 1881, Charles Field retired and the firm of E. Gerard, Dufraisseix et Morel took over management with Charles Field retaining a silent partnership and using the backstamp mark of CFH/GDM. Around 1900, Morel left the firm and Frank Abbott, their American distributor in New York City, became a partner, hence the backstamp change to CFH/GDA.

Robert Haviland, the grandson of Charles Field, started his own china manufacturing business, *Haviland et Le Tanneur*, in 1924 with his brother-in-law Pierre Le Tanneur. He was able to purchase the Charles Field Haviland backmark from the Gerard and Abbott company in 1941, and with C. Parlon in 1949, established the firm of Robert Haviland et C. Parlon.

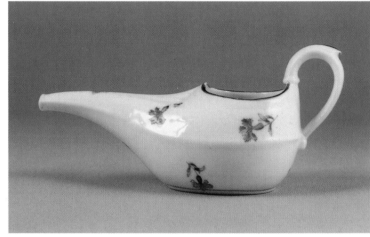

Figure 6. Invalid feeder, factory decorated. Charles Field Haviland, backstamp CFH/GDM, 1882-1890. *Courtesy of Marty Tackitt.* $75-150.

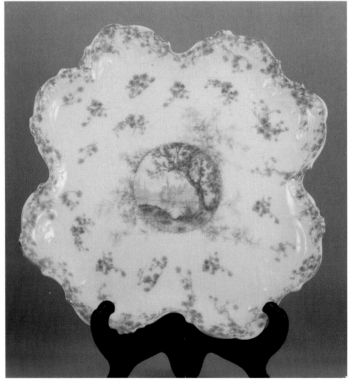

Figure 7. Cookie tray in unidentified pattern and blank. Charles Field Haviland, backstamp CFH/GDM, 1882-1890. *Courtesy of R & J Mairs.* $75-135.

Figure 8. Cookie tray with unglazed bottom in unidentified pattern on Schleiger no. 1274. (Please refer to information regarding Schleiger numbers under section on Place Setting Pieces and Identification: Locating a Pattern) Charles Field Haviland, backstamp CFH/GDA, after 1900. $75-125.

Figure 9. Coffee pot in unclassified pattern. Charles Field Haviland, backstamp CFH/GDA, after 1900. $125-250.

Johann Haviland

Jean Haviland was the son of Charles Edward Haviland and the grandson of David Haviland. In 1907, he started his own firm in Bavaria, Germany, under the name of Johann Haviland. By 1924, this company was no longer in business and the rights to the name had been bought by an Italian manufacturing company, Richard-Ginori, who owned the Johann Haviland Company until 1933.

In 1937, the German porcelain manufacturer, Rosenthal, bought the company. If it is operating today with the name Johann Haviland, it is probably part of the Rosenthal Cartel which owns almost all of the German and Austrian porcelain companies such as Heutschenreuter. Johann Haviland china has no connection with the French or American Haviland china.

Figure 10. Coffee pot, cup and saucer in Blue Garland pattern. Johann Haviland, Bavarian, circa 1960-1980s. $75-125.

Part 2:
The Making of Haviland China

Whiteware: Glazed Undecorated White Porcelain

In 1709 true, or hard paste, porcelain was discovered in Europe by a Berlin apothecary's apprentice named Johann Friedrich Böttger. Augustus the Strong, king of Poland and elector of Saxony, became Böttger's protector and funded the first project at Meissen (Dresden) in 1710, filling the royal coffers with money as the demand for porcelain grew throughout Europe.

Prior to that time, most of the porcelain had been imported from China. The French and Italians had tried some experiments with artificial soft paste porcelain but were not very successful. They tried to copy the Chinese porcelain, but were mistakenly led to believe that the translucent quality was created by adding powdered glass to the mixture of sand and pipe clay. This soft paste porcelain was beautiful but impractical; it broke easily and did not measure up to the quality of hard paste porcelain.

The secret for making hard paste porcelain was jealously guarded at Meissen, but in the course of time that knowledge was bound to leak out. A prize catch for rival china manufacturers was a dissatisfied workman who left the Meissen factory with information regarding the production of porcelain.

The primary material used for hard paste porcelain is called kaolin, a clay that comes from the decomposition of granite and which is only available in a few places in the world. Kaolin gives porcelain that special quality not found in ordinary pottery, earthenware, or soft paste porcelain.

Porcelain is vitreous, which means the glaze cannot be penetrated and therefore is impervious to liquids. It is light weight, translucent and delicate, yet at the same time, strong and durable.

Kaolin was discovered in Limoges, France, around 1770, marking the beginning of Limoges as the center of the porcelain industry in Europe. Prior to the French Revolution, the state-owned Sevres Factory was the major porcelain manufacturer. When Napoleon I came to power, he gave control back to the various old Parisian manufacturers who then moved their plants to Limoges for easy access to the clay. In 1807, there were approximately 200 workers in the city; by 1830 that number had increased to 1,800.

Once a paste of white kaolin, quartzose sand and feldspar had been mixed, pieces were thrown by hand. Cups were thrown on an ancient kick-wheel, while plates were made with a plaster mold and then placed on the wheel. Larger items were made with three-part plaster molds made in pieces and assembled later using paste and water. When the items were completely dried, they were fired at 1000 degrees Celsius, which caused the porcelain to become hard and porous. They were then dipped in glaze, a mixture of quartz and feldspar, and fired again at 1800 degrees Celsius (3200 degrees Fahrenheit). After this process, the porcelain was then sent to the decorative shop for design, stacked on wooden planks and carried on the heads or shoulders of plank carriers.

The earliest blanks, or shapes, were sculptured into simple classic forms, sometimes with squash or other vegetables as finials. The majority of pieces were of a heavier weight. In 1865, Charles Edward Haviland introduced blanks that were of a more delicate nature; Crystal, Ruby, and Argent. With the advent of more sophisticated machinery, the shapes of the blanks also became more ornate and varied. The catalog of 1879 lists the following shapes: Cable, Ovide, Parisian, Anchor, Saxon, Nenuphar (Waterlily), Sevres, English, Coupe, Japanese, Laced, Rose, Boule, Butterfly, Yedo, Normand and Monaco. The catalog dates seem to run from 1864 to 1878 for these shapes.

Prior to 1890, teapots and oval items had been molded. It was then discovered that by mixing sodium silicate into the paste, the porcelain was then fluid enough to be cast. With this casting process, Haviland was able to create fine, translucent shapes that fascinated the public.

The Japanese influence (1870-1880) was felt strongly in the undecorated porcelain whiteware as well as in the decorative ware, especially with the Napkin Fold and Cannelé blanks. In the 1880s and 1890s, new blanks came into production while old ones were discontinued. The Marseille blank was a very important shape, as well as the Ranson blank, which was designed by Paul Ranson, a factory painter from 1890 to 1893.

Figure 11. Waste bowl, used for dregs of tea leaves and lemon, on plain blank. Haviland & Company, 1876-1889, Mark F. $35-65.

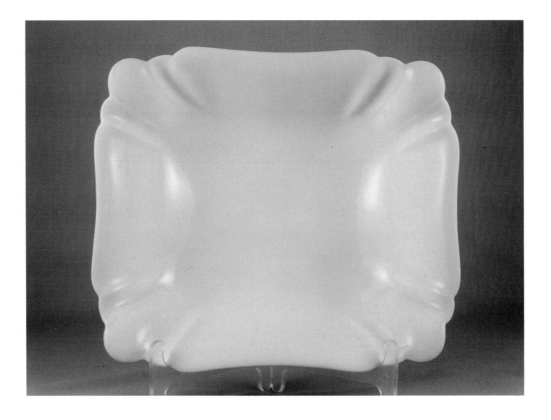

Figure 12. Open serving bowl, Henri II blank, Schleiger no. 10. Haviland & Company, 1888-1896, Mark H. $75-125.

Figure 13. Open oval vegetable bowl in Cannelé blank, Schleiger no. 413. Haviland & Company, 1888-1896, Mark H. $85-150.

Figure 14. Salad plate in *Ranson* blank. Haviland & Company, 1893-1931, Mark I. $20-35.

Decorative Ware

Varied styles of *Old Paris* porcelain made up a large part of the decorative patterns in the early Haviland years. These were hand painted with a solid gold band or various solid colors outlined in gold, used prior to the introduction of engraved transfer mono-chrome outlines in 1855. During the late 1850s, Moss Rose and other single flowers or bouquets appeared in the center of the plates. These flowers have been found to be entirely hand painted or hand painted "fill-ins" (the engraved transfers at that time were only black outlines and the colors were painted within the lines).

Figure 15. Large serving bowl from set in *Old Paris* style. Haviland & Company, 1853, Mark A. *Courtesy of Marty Tackitt.* $150-300.

Figure 16. Covered sauce dish on attached underplate with molded squash finial. Haviland & Company, 1853, Mark A. Only three pieces in the entire set have backstamp, as the incised stamp was placed just on larger, heavier pieces. Also, Haviland did not mark all of their dinnerware until 1871. If an early piece looks like Haviland but has no mark, it might be from a large set that had only a few backstamps; however, without that backstamp, it is difficult to definitely verify the piece was made by Haviland. $150-300.

Figure 17. A relish dish from the same burgundy set. Haviland & Company, 1853, Mark A. $75-125.

Figure 18. One of a set of 8 lunch plates and part of the molded squash set. The small ring in center is similar to Wedding Ring pattern that Haviland made in gold trim. The burgundy band was not common, most were of gold or green. Haviland & Company, 1853, Mark A. Complete set with serving pieces $2,500-4,000.

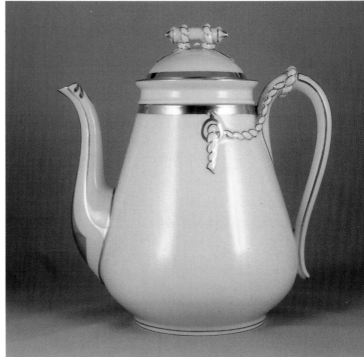

Figure 19. *Pôt de Créme* tiered tray and covered cups. Haviland & Company, 1853, Mark A. $400-700.

Figure 20. Large coffee pot in the cable shape with gold trim. Haviland & Company, 1876-1889, Marks F and g. $125-250.

Figure 21. One pound sugar bowl and creamer in the cable shape with gold trim. Haviland & Company, 1876-1889, Marks F and g. $95-150 set.

Figure 22. Round covered serving bowl in the cable shape with gold trim. The gold on the earlier pieces was of a bright, brassy gold. Haviland & Company, 1876-1889, Marks F and g. $95-150.

Figure 23. Old Wedding Ring cups and saucers. *Left to right*: Very large Café au Lait cup, heavy crockery tea cup and standard tea cup made of very thin porcelain. A wedding ring design is in the bottom of each cup. Some people incorrectly call the later gold bands of 1894-1931 by this name. Haviland & Company, 1876-1889, Marks F and g. $32-65.

Figure 24. Old Wedding Ring cake plate. Haviland & Company, 1876-1889, Marks F and g. $75-125.

Figure 25. Large water or milk pitcher and small cups with legs and feet on a base, very unusual pattern. These cups may be for drinking, none of the catalogs available show this item. Haviland & Company, 1865, Mark B. *Courtesy of Marty Tackitt.* Cups, each $50-150; Pitcher $175-300.

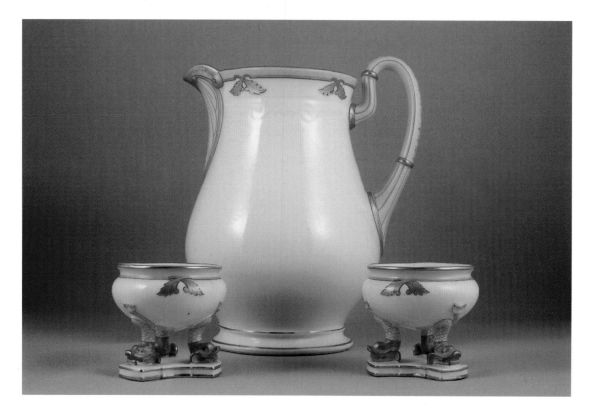

Figure 26. Large tea pot, factory decorated. Haviland & Company, 1853, Mark A. *Courtesy of Marty Tackitt.* $175-250.

Figure 27. Coffee pot with cup and saucer, factory decorated. Haviland & Company, 1865, Mark B. *Courtesy of Marty Tackitt.* $175-250.

Figure 28. Large water pitcher in Moss Rose with gold trim, in Ivy blank. Haviland & Company, 1876-1886, Mark D. *Courtesy of Marty Tackitt.* $150-300.

Under Charles Edward's leadership and modernization, new blanks and designs were created. By hiring the best contemporary artists of the time — Bracquemond, Dammouse, Boilvin, etc — Charles Edward was able to keep in the forefront of design. Designs in shape and decoration went from Rococo to Renaissance Revival to Japanesque.

With the opening of trade doors into Japan in 1853, an entirely new style appeared in Europe and the United States. Everything had a Japanese motif, including Haviland china. Adaptation of these designs into Western styling during the 1870s and 1880s created for Haviland a reputation of excellence in porcelain making.

Prior to the Asian influence, the patterns had been either geometric on the plate, mostly on the rim, or a simple flower or two in the center. With the Japanese influence, however, the patterns flowed across the entire surface of the plate.

Figure 30. Dessert plate in Olive Dammouse, 8½". Haviland & Company, 1876-1889, Marks F and c. *Courtesy of R & J Mairs.* $65-125.

Figure 29. Salad plate in Moss Rose with pink trim. Moss Rose came with several different colored borders. Haviland & Company, 1876-1889, Marks F and g. $20-35.

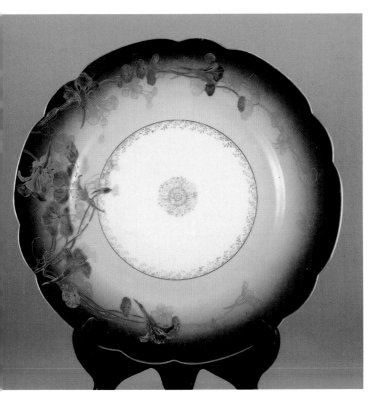

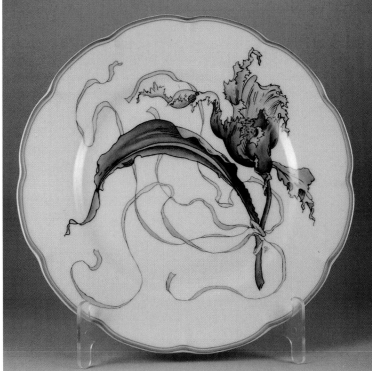

Figure 31. Dessert plate in Turquoise Dammouse. Haviland & Company, 1876-1889, Marks F and c. *Courtesy of R & J Mairs.* $65-125.

Figure 32. *Orchidee* (Orchid), First Issue in Series *Fleuer & Ribbon*, Limited Edition Plate from an original design created by Felix Bracquemond. Signed by Frederick Haviland, 1986, Mark Q. $50-95.

Figure 33. *Hiver* (Winter) in the series *Théâtre des Saisons*, Limited Edition Plate from an original design created by Felix Bracquemond. Signed by Frederick Haviland, 1986, Mark Q. $50-95.

Along with the transfers, some hand painting was also done, particularly brush strokes of white enameling for accent on the more expensive pieces. The Auteuil Studio artists, under the leadership of Felix Bracquemond, gave Haviland a broad range of art, from Oriental to Impressionistic. They created Japanese figures, marine and animal scenes, birds and flowers; all of which were then made into transfers and placed on fish and game sets, comports and other decorative table pieces.

Figure 35. Top of comport showing oriental design. Haviland & Company, 1894-1931, Marks I and c. $125-225.

Figure 34. Demitasse cup and saucer with oriental design. Haviland & Company, 1894-1931, Marks I and c. *Courtesy of Marty Tackitt.* $35-65.

Figure 36. Side view of comport in Fig. 35.

Figure 37. Large round covered casserole in Anchor shape, factory decorated with oriental and floral design. Haviland & Company, 1876-1889, Marks F and g. *Courtesy of Marty Tackitt.* $125-250.

Figure 38. Old Blackberry luncheon plate, Schleiger no. 1154E on napkinfold blank. Haviland & Company, 1876-1889, Marks F and g. $65-95.

Figure 39. Old Blackberry salad bowl, Schleiger no. 1154. Haviland & Company, 1876-1889, Marks F and g. $125-175.

Figure 40. Bacon platter in *Old Carnation* pattern, Schleiger no. 1158A on blank no. 10, 8" x 9½". This comes in blue and pink as well. Haviland & Company, 1876-1889, Marks F and c. $65-125.

Figure 41. 8½" coupe dessert plate in unidentified pattern on Torse blank, Schleiger no. 413. Haviland & Company, 1887, Mark G. $30-50.

Charles Edward Haviland, with his love for impressionistic painting, encouraged his artists to be creative in their designs. These designs were reflected in the variety of subject matter along with balance of color and form. Several of the floral patterns created also reflected this freedom. In comparing the same design on two plates of the same set, seldom are they exactly alike. This is because the artisan applying the transfers did not always place them exactly in the same way on every piece. With all of the new improvements in porcelain manufacturing, the factories today still rely on the human touch to produce the final product; gold trim and handles painted by hand with the artist's touch.

Some of the plates from the 1920s and 1930s were decorated with a creme border of a translucent overglaze. This gave a distinctive look to the china; however, as the creme border faded in bright light, this treatment was not successful. If these plates were displayed in a china cabinet in a sun-lit room, the creme slowly faded away.

With the beginning of the Art Deco movement, William Haviland brought Jean Dufy, Kandinsky, Suzanne Lalique, Eduoard Sandoz and other designers into the company to design for him. They created modernistic, cheerful patterns to fit on the simplified shapes. Fussy and frilly were out. Designs to this day are bright, bold and contemporary.

Figure 42. Ginger jar in *Cathay*. Haviland & Company, circa 1970-1980. $125-200.

Unusual and Collectible Haviland

Meadow Visitor

During the 1880s, with the Asian influence, there was a fascination with birds and butterflies as decoration. Haviland & Company designed several combinations of birds, butterflies and flowers to create a pattern listed in their 1879 Catalog as *Foins et Papillons*, translated as *Hay and Butterflies*, now commonly known in America as *Meadow Visitors*. This common name may have evolved with some Haviland matcher or antique dealer; company records are silent on the term. Within one set, every plate could possibly have a unique bird and butterfly, each flying in a different direction than the last.

Meadow Visitor is listed in the 1879 Catalog and possibly dates into the early 1870s as Haviland & Company placed this pattern on several varied blanks and on unusual pieces. Charles Field Haviland also produced several pieces in *Meadow Visitors*. Here are just a few of the treatments for this interesting pattern.

Figure 43. Luncheon plate with Meadow Visitor design on Torse blank. Haviland & Company, 1876-1886, Marks D and g. $30-50.

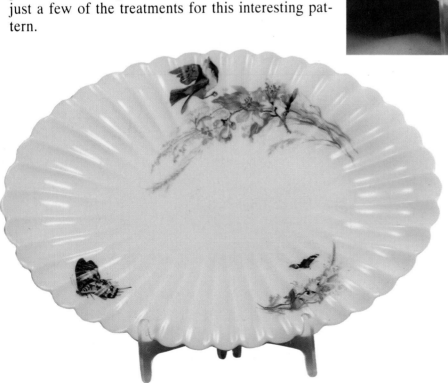

Figure 44. 14" platter in Meadow Visitor design on Torse blank. Haviland & Company, 1876-1886, Marks D and g. $125-175.

Figure 45. Meadow Visitor luncheon plate on Wheat, plain shape. Haviland & Company, 1876-1886, Marks D and g. $30-50.

Figure 46. Individual ice cream plate in Meadow Visitor on leaf blank. Haviland & Company, 1876-1889, Marks F and g. $95-145.

Figure 47. Individual butter dish in Meadow Visitor, smooth blank, Schleiger no. 1155. Haviland & Company, 1876-1879, Marks D and g. *Courtesy of R & J Mairs.* $25-30.

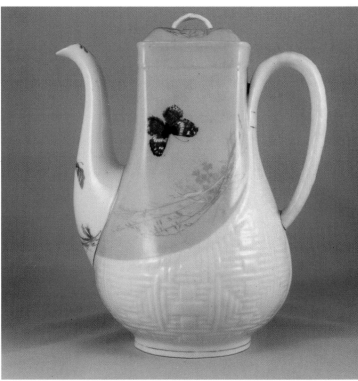

Figure 48. Sauce boat in Meadow Visitor pattern on unusual blank. Haviland & Company, 1876-1886, Marks D and g. $100-125.

Figure 49. Meadow Visitor coffee pot on Osier blank with pink background. Haviland & Company, 1886-1889, Marks D and g. $250-350.

Figure 50. Meadow Visitor salad plate, tea cup and saucer on smooth blank with pink background. Haviland & Company, 1886-1889, Marks D and g. Plate $30-40, Cup/saucer $50-60.

Figure 51. Invalid feeder in Meadow Visitor on Osier blank. Haviland & Company, 1877-1883, Marks E and d. *Courtesy of Marty Tackitt.* $150-200.

Figure 52. Creamer on Osier blank in different version of Meadow Visitor, factory decorated in brown and gold. Haviland & Company, 1876-1889, Mark F and g. $60-75.

Figure 53. Handled sauce boat with attached underplate in Meadow Visitor variation. Haviland & Company, 1876-1889, Marks D and g. *Courtesy of Marty Tackitt.* $125-150.

Figure 54. Tea cup and saucer in unusual Meadow Visitor design. Haviland & Company, 1876-1889, Marks C and g. *Courtesy of Marty Tackitt.* $65-95.

Figure 55. Bacon platter with Meadow Visitor trim and bold floral design in center. Haviland & Company, 1876-1889, Marks D and g. *Courtesy of Marty Tackitt.* $200-225.

Figure 56. Top of comport, showing orange and blossoms in center of plate with Meadow Visitor edge. Haviland & Company, 1876-1889, Marks D and g. *Courtesy of Marty Tackitt.* $250-350.

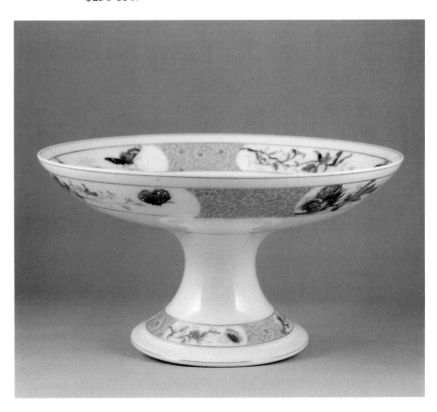

Figure 57. Side view of comport in Fig. 56.

Feu de Four

Haviland & Company was always looking for new ways to be creative. Having mastered the technique of glazing and firing, Charles Edward Haviland decided to try something innovative. Transfers could have been placed either under or on top of the glaze, but Jean d'Albis suggests in his book that the transfers were placed on top with an additional firing at the foot of the kiln where the temperature is lower. The word *Four* refers to the main whiteware kiln and not to the muffle kiln normally used for the firing of transfers.

Flowers and colors varied, but they all have the soft, muted tones that identify this process. The main pattern found is a poppy pattern called *Flowers and seeds*, although a few other patterns were done as well. The patterns were done on several different blanks and gold trims.

Since this process was very expensive to create, the china must have been very costly. The scarcity of *Feu de Four* on the market in recent years indicates that it must have had little commercial appeal because of the high price, however it is much in demand among collectors today.

Some reference books have given 1893 to 1895 as the years of production, but pieces of *Feu de Four* have been found on Schleiger blank no. 19, which was not patented until 1903.

Figure 58. *Feu de Four* chocolate pot with cobalt and gold trim on Schleiger blank no. 4. Haviland & Company, 1893-1931, Marks H and h. *Courtesy of Marty Tackitt.* $350-500.

Figure 59. *Feu de Four* ice relish 5" on Ranson blank with gold no. 24. Haviland & Company, 1893-1931, Marks I, c and h. $85-125.

Figure 60. *Feu de Four* berry bowl, 9". Haviland & Company, 1893-1931, Marks I and h. $200-$250.

Figure 61. Dessert plate, 8½", from set of ten, on Ranson blank with elaborate gold trim. The plate also has gold on the underbase rim. The backstamp does not say *Feu de Four,* but compare the berry bowl in Fig. 60 which has correct backstamp, floral patterns and coloring are identical. Haviland & Company, 1894-1931, Marks I and c. $100-150 ea.

Cobalt and Red Decorative Pieces

Cobalt is fired in exactly the same manner as *Feu de Four,* and considered to this day to be one of the most expensive porcelains. At the Haviland factory in Limoges in 1992, a cup and saucer in cobalt and gold trim sold for over $400.00. The majority of Haviland porcelain is decorated *over* the glaze. However, cobalt is placed *under* the glaze with the gold trim as decoration over the glaze. The original catalog refers to Cobalt in French as *Bleu de Four.*

Only the very wealthy could have afforded entire sets of this elaborate china. Royal houses of Europe would possibly have used them for state dinners and American "royalty" would have coveted them as well.

The red decorative pieces are placed in this section as they were also very expensive to create, but were done in the normal way, not double-fired.

Figure 62. Ice cream platter, factory painted with cobalt and gold trim. Haviland & Company, 1887-1889, Marks G and g. *Courtesy of Marty Tackitt.* $275-375.

Figure 63. Salad plate in Schleiger no. 140 with cobalt and gold trim on blank no. 126. Theodore Haviland, 1893, Mark L. $65-75.

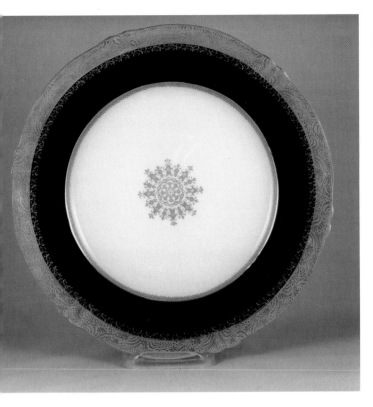

Figure 64. Dinner plate in cobalt and gold. Theodore Haviland, 1903, Mark p. $75-95.

Figure 66. Elegant dinner plate in cobalt and gold on Ranson blank. Haviland & Company, Marks H and c plus H & Co. 1893 in gold. *Courtesy of Marty Tackitt.* $95-150.

Figure 65. After-dinner coffee cup and saucer in unidentified cobalt and gold pattern. Theodore Haviland, 1903, Mark p. $90-100.

Figure 67. Chocolate cup and saucer in cobalt and gold with floral center, Ranson blank. Haviland & Company, 1888-1896, Marks H & c. *Courtesy of Marty Tackitt* $90-125.

Figure 68. Dinner plate in cobalt fading to pale blue with gold emblem at top, in Marseille shape. Haviland & Company, 1876-1879, Mark C. *Courtesy of Marty Tackitt.* $95-150.

Figure 70. Individual butter dish in cobalt and gold. Haviland & Company, 1876-1889, Marks F and g. *Courtesy of Marty Tackitt.* $35-40.

Figure 69. Chocolate cup and saucer with cobalt and gold trim in blank no. 204 and unidentified pattern. Haviland & Company, 1894-1931, Marks I and c. *Courtesy of Marty Tackitt.* $75-95.

Figure 71. Large relish dish in cobalt and gold by Dammouse, 8" x 10". Haviland & Company, 1876-1879, Mark C. *Courtesy of Marty Tackitt.* $325-425.

Figure 72. Charger with handles, 12", cobalt and gold trim. Haviland & Company, 1894-1903, Marks I and c. *Courtesy of Marty Tackitt.* $225-325.

Figure 73. Cracker jar with underplate, cobalt and gold. Charles Field Haviland, CFH/GDM, 1882-1891. *Courtesy of Marty Tackitt.* $250-325.

Figure 74. Top of comport, factory painted with cobalt and gold trim. Charles Field Haviland, CFH/GDM, 1882-1891. *Courtesy of Marty Tackitt.* $225-275.

Figure 75. Side view of comport in Fig. 74.

Figure 76. Large serving bowl with cobalt and gold. Charles Field Haviland, CFH/GDM, 1882-1891. *Courtesy of Marty Tackitt.* $250-350.

Figure 77. Unusual serving bowl in red and gold on Schleiger blank no. 208. Haviland & Company, 1887, Marks G & c. *Courtesy of Marty Tackitt.* $250-350.

Figure 78. Dinner plate in red and gold on Ranson blank. Haviland & Company, 1888-1896, Marks H and c. *Courtesy of Marty Tackitt.* $125-175.

Figure 79. Bone dish, 3¼" x 6", in an unidentified pattern, deep color fading into lighter shade in crescent shape. Haviland & Company, 1876-1889, Marks F and c. $25-35.

Figure 80. Jardiniere or flower vase, 5½" x 9½", in the Marseille shape, Schleiger no. 9, in rust with undercolor of beige. Old catalogs show bowl on a large scalloped tray, however most trays did not survive because they were so fragile. Haviland & Company, 1876-1889, Marks F and c. $225-325.

Display and Portrait Pieces

Figure 81. *Murmures d'Amours*, 12" charger, factory decorated. Haviland & Company, 1894-1900, Marks I and c. *Courtesy of Marty Tackitt.* $800-1000.

With entertaining reaching its most elaborate by 1890, both Haviland companies hired the best artists to create dessert ware and magnificent works of art for display. These pieces, reminiscent of work done by the Meissen and Sevres factories years before, placed the Havilands at the top of their field.

Fish and game sets were the largest example of the factory art work, but dessert sets were also popular. However, some pieces were so unusual in design and concept that they were used for display purposes only. Some sets contained complete themes with each plate telling part of the story, sometimes with text written on the back of the plate.

The two busts shown in this section, are an example of the creativity and talent of artists hired by the Haviland companies. The "Jenny Lind" bust was one of the pieces Haviland & Company displayed at the 1855 Paris Exposition where they won the silver medal.

Figure 82. *Fleurs Ecloses*, dessert plate, factory decorated. Haviland & Company, 1894-1900, Marks I and c. *Courtesy of Marty Tackitt.* $350-450.

Figure 83. *Chasse Louis XV*, dessert plate, factory decorated. Haviland & Company, 1894-1900, Marks I and c. *Courtesy of Marty Tackitt.* $350-450.

Figure 84. *Mde D. St. d'Angouleine*, 8½" dessert plate, hand painted and signed by factory artist, L. Jean, with elaborate cobalt and gold border. Theodore Haviland, 1892, Mark K. $250-350.

opposite page:
Figure 85. Pauline Bonaparte, from a set of Napoleon's Ladies. This set consists of a 12" charger with Napoleon's picture in center and twelve dessert plates decorated with different women in his life. This set has cobalt and gold trim. Mary Gaston's book, *Haviland Collectables & Objects of Art*, shows the set with gold on white. Theodore Haviland, hand painted and signed by L. Jean, 1895, Mark m. Complete set $3500-4000.

left:
Figure 86. Mme Roland, one from set of Napoleon's Ladies.

Figure 87. One of twelve luncheon or dessert plates in unusual Egyptian design, with six different scenes repeated twice throughout the set. Each scene shows some aspect of fishing; boats, fish nets, fish in barrels, etc. These plates were probably part of a fish set. Charles Field Haviland, 1882-1890, backmark CFH/GDM. Complete set $1250-1500.

Figure 89. From Egyptian set.

Figure 88. From Egyptian set.

Figure 90. From Egyptian set.

Figure 91. From Egyptian set.

Figure 93. Tea cup with factory decorated scenes on four different panels plus ornate gold trim. Haviland & Company, 1888, Marks H and c. $75-95.

Figure 92. From Egyptian set.

Figure 94. Wheel barrow scenic plate with cobalt and gold trim, factory hand painted. Haviland & Company, 1887-1889, Marks G and g. *Courtesy of Marty Tackitt.* $225-300.

Figure 95. 8½" dessert plate with flowers in foreground and different scenes in background, from set of four. Haviland & Company, 1894-1904, Marks I and c. *Courtesy of Marty Tackitt.* $125-175.

Figure 96. 8½" dessert plate with flowers and garlands and different scenes in background, from set of four. Haviland & Company, 1894-1904, Marks I and c. *Courtesy of Marty Tackitt.* $125-175.

Figure 97. Covered casserole in Marseille blank. Factory painted with angels, blue background and yellow panels. Haviland & Company, 1876-1878, Marks F and c. *Courtesy of Marty Tackitt.* $275-350.

Figure 98. Dinner plate with factory painted cherubs on floral background of Schleiger no. 221 on blank no. 25. Haviland & Company, 1888-1903, Marks H and c. *Courtesy of Marty Tackitt.* $125-225.

Figure 99. *Longfellow's Song of Hiawatha*, painted and signed by factory artist C. Piton. Dessert plate is number five in series of twelve. Haviland & Company, 1876-1886, Marks D and g. $225-300.

Figure 100. Back view of *Song of Hiawatha.* Plates 1 through 12 tell the story of Hiawatha with portion of the poem on back of each plate. This one reads *"Thus departed Hiawatha, Hiawatha the Beloved, In the glory of the sunset, In the purple mists of Evening. Hiawatha's departure XXII."* There is a small numeral 5 at top of plate, indicating fifth in series.

Figure 101. Sculpture, 7", *"Jewess of Algiers,"* signed by factory artist L. Savine. Theodore Haviland, 1904, Mark p. *Courtesy of HCIF, Art Wendt, Photographer.* $1500-2500.

Figure 102. Bust, 9", *"Jenny Lind,"* attributed to Magnus, a German artist. Haviland & Company, 1855, Mark B. *Courtesy of HCIF, Art Wendt, Photographer.* $7500-9000.

Sandoz

From 1915 to 1920, Edouard Sandoz, of the Sandoz Pharmaceutical family, designed unusual shapes of animals and people for Theodore Haviland Company. Cats, bulldogs, birds, fish, frogs, rabbits, clowns, etc., were turned into coffee pots, vases, knife rests, pitchers of all sizes, salt and pepper sets and other interesting pieces. Today, these collectibles are bringing high prices.

In the 1970s, Haviland reproduced some of the more popular Sandoz animals and figures for Tiffany & Company. These are plainly marked as reproductions and are worth a tenth of the original pieces.

Figure 103. Salt and pepper shakers designed and signed by Sandoz. Theodore Haviland, 1915-1920. *Courtesy of Marty Tackitt.* $400-600.

Figure 104. Frog (ashtray?), 2½" tall with 5½" x 6" base. Theodore Haviland, Mark p and signed by Sandoz, 1915-1920. *Courtesy of Art Wendt, Photographer.* $300-500.

Figure 105. *Téte à Téte set,* small coffee pot with two cups on a tray, one of many animals designed by Edouard Sandoz. Theodore Haviland, 1915-1920, Marks O and p. $1000-1500.

Figure 106. Two chocolate cups and saucers designed by Edouard Sandoz. Theodore Haviland, 1915-1920, Marks O and p. Each $75-100.

Figure 107. Salt and pepper shakers in the *Montmery* pattern, designed by Sandoz and incised with his initials. Haviland & Company, Mark I and c, 1894-1931. *Courtesy of Art Wendt, photographer.* $300-500.

For Bed and Bath

China pieces were used throughout the house, not just at meal time. Haviland & Company found a ready market with porcelain pieces for the dressing table, the night stand and the washstand or bathroom. They were strong and durable, as well as beautiful.

Some of the items, such as the candlesticks, match box and dresser sets, were of the same porcelain used to make dinnerware, mugs, chamber pots, wash basins and pitchers were of a heavier weight. Not many of these pieces were made after 1900.

Figure 108. Candlesticks on Marseille blank, *Dresden* pattern Schleiger no. 679D. Haviland & Company, 1879-1889, Marks H and d. *Courtesy of Marty Tackitt.* Pair $250-300.

Figure 109. Match box, part of set in Fig. 108. Haviland & Company, 1879-1889, Marks H and d. *Courtesy of Marty Tackitt.* $250-300.

Figure 110. Chamberstick with *"Sweet Dreams"* printed and navy blue trim. Haviland & Company, 1876-1889, Marks F and g. *Courtesy of Marty Tackitt.* $145-165.

Figure 111. Dresser tray in variation of Schleiger no. 670, on Ranson blank with ornate gold, unglazed bottom. Haviland & Company, 1888-1903, Marks H and c. $125-150.

Figure 112. Dresser tray with pomade and puff boxes (lids are missing), in variation of Schleiger no. 670. (Note: Lids were fired with base to get perfect fit. If rim is rough and unglazed, item should have lid). Complete set $375-450.

Figure 113. Ring holder in variation of Schleiger no. 478. Haviland & Company, 1876-1896, Marks H and a. $125-175.

Figure 114. Pin tray in variation of Schleiger no. 735A. Haviland & Company, 1893-1931, marks I and c. $95-125.

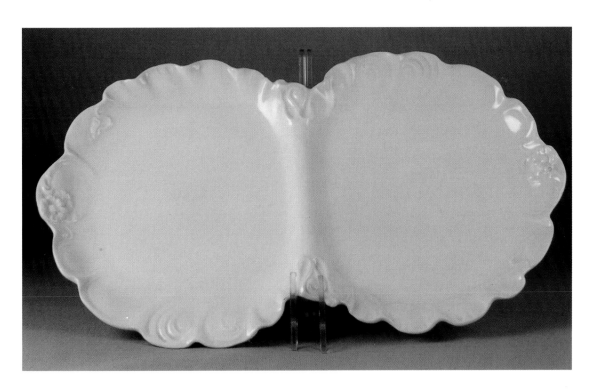

Figure 115. Dresser tray in Charles Field Haviland, CFH/GDM, 1882-1891. $125-175.

Figure 116. Wash pitcher and basin in Cobalt Blue with gold design, rare. Wash pitcher is 11" tall and 8" at widest part, bowl is 15½" wide and 5½" tall. Haviland & Company, 1876-1889. Pitcher has Mark I and is numbered, the bowl has Mark F with Mark c on both. *Courtesy of Art Wendt, Photographer.* Set $2000-3000.

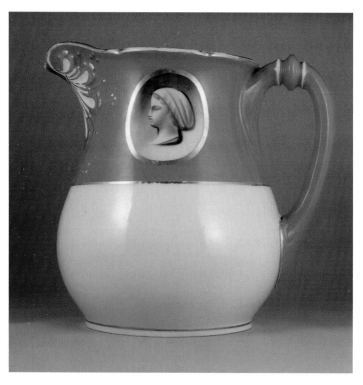

Figure 117. Water pitcher. Haviland & Company, 1865, Mark B. *Courtesy of Marty Tackitt.* $250-400.

Figure 118. Lady's spit cup, factory decorated. This was part of a Lady's toilette set. After brushing her teeth, she would rinse her mouth and spit into the cup. Haviland & Company, 1879-1889, Mark g. *Courtesy of Marty Tackitt.* $125-150.

Figure 119. Tall toothbrush holder and covered toothbrush holder in Moss Rose with dark blue trim. Haviland & Company, 1876-1889, Marks C and g. *Courtesy of Marty Tackitt.* Tall holder $125-150, covered holder $150-165.

Figure 120. Covered soap dish and two sizes of shaving mugs. Haviland & Company, 1865, Mark B. *Courtesy of Marty Tackitt.* Left to right: $125-175, $95-150, $85-125.

Figure 121. Child's chamber pot. Haviland & Company, 1894-1931, Mark I with a decorator mark of Jean Luce, Paris and a rectangle logo. $125-225.

Railroad China

With the advent of the railroad, people began to enjoy traveling, and the best part of the trip was eating in the dining car. Meals were seldom eaten in restaurants, especially by the middle class, so it was a special treat to dine on the train.

Gourmet meals were served on fine china with beautiful crystal, silver serving pieces and elegant table linens. Ordinary fine china could not withstand the bumping and shaking of a train, therefore the various railroads commissioned china manufacturers to produce sturdy railroad china that would still have that *fine china* look. A few pieces, such as tea cups and saucers, were made of thin porcelain; however, they were not normally used on the train, but given as souvenirs to ladies who were called upon to serve afternoon tea.

Both Haviland & Company and Theodore Haviland made railroad china, but to be officially considered as *Railroad China*, the china needs to have the proper identifying backstamps of the railroad lines for which they were commissioned, as the Haviland companies also produced the same patterns in regular dinnerware.

Figure 122. Bread boat in Schleiger no. 491, from the Missouri Pacific Railroad. Haviland & Company, 1894-1931, Mark I. *Courtesy of Marty Tackitt.* $250-400.

Figure 123. Bacon platter in Schleiger no. 240 variation, made for Burley & Company, expressly for the New York Central Lines. Haviland & Company, 1894-1931, Marks I and c. *Courtesy of Marty Tackitt.* $200-350.

Figure 124. Tea cup and saucer used on the Chicago-Milwaukee & St. Paul Railway, also reads "to Puget Sound, Electrified." Given to ladies who were called upon to serve afternoon tea on the train. Theodore Haviland, 1894-1903, Marks M and q. $125-150.

Club/Hotel Ware, Advertising China and Smoking Accessories

The better restaurants, hotels and clubs catered to the elite and used only the finest china. Haviland made dinnerware for several of these establishments, customizing the china with their special logos or names. Some of the dinnerware was of a heavier quality, similar to railroad china.

Ashtrays were, and still are, a popular form of advertising, and more than one Haviland ashtray probably found its way home in someone's pocket. Some, such as the one from the American Embassy in Paris, were possibly given as mementos.

Cigarettes have been around for a long time and ceramic pieces with reference to smoking were made by the Haviland companies. Here is just a sampling of interesting smoking accessories. There were small quantities of these pieces made, so they are very rare today.

Figure 126. Salad plate in club/hotel ware from the Hotel St. Louis et de la Poste. The carriage route from Paris to Nice is shown with the hotel at top and each carriage labeled with the four locations on the route; Nice, Paris, Valence, and Saulieu. Theodore Haviland, 1926-1936, Marks P and r. $75-95.

Figure 125. Club/Hotel Ware. Tea cup, saucer and salad plate from the Fairmont Hotel. Logo in center of plate and on side of cup. Theodore Haviland, 1903, Mark p. *Courtesy of Marty Tackitt.* $125-150.

Figure 127. Egg cup, open on both ends, from a hotel in France. Theodore Haviland, 1936-1962, Marks P and R. *Courtesy of Marty Tackitt.* $75-125.

Figure 128. After-dinner coffee cup and saucer from the Pink Poodle Restaurant in San Francisco. Cup is turned to show poodle in front of cup. Haviland & Company, 1894-1931, Marks I and c. *Courtesy of Marty Tackitt.* $125-175.

Figure 129. Ashtray made especially for G.H. Mumm & Company for Gordon Rouge Champagne. Haviland & Company, 1894-1931, Marks I, c and i. *Courtesy of Marty Tackitt.* $75-150.

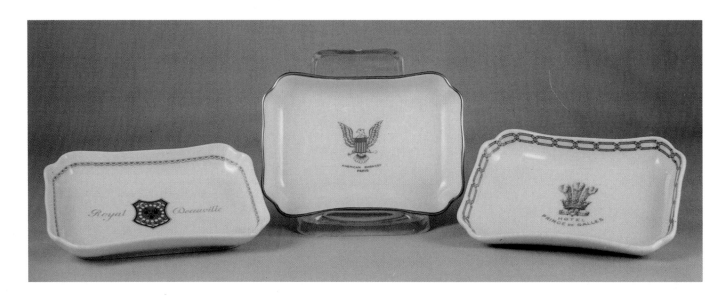

Figure 130. Ashtrays made especially for various restaurants, hotels and organizations: *From left*, Hotel Royal Deauville; American Embassy, Paris; and Hotel Prince de Galles. Theodore Haviland, 1936-1945, Marks I and P. each $65-75.

Figure 131. After-dinner coffee and ashtray set, 5½" x 3¼". Theodore Haviland, 1925-1945, Marks P and r. *Courtesy of Marty Tackitt.* $125-225.

Figure 132. Match holder and strike. Charles Field Haviland, CFH/GDA, 1900-1941. *Courtesy of Marty Tackitt.* $125-200.

Figure 133. Match box holder with opening on side to strike, hand painted. Haviland & Company, 1894-1931, Mark I. *Courtesy of Marty Tackitt.* $150-225.

Figure 134. Ash tray with horse motif, 8" round. Theodore Haviland, 1958-1962, Marks R and s. *Courtesy of Marty Tackitt.* $125-165.

69

Pottery, Stoneware and Porcelain Vases

Haviland made porcelain vases from the early years of production, but became more creative in stoneware and pottery between 1876 and 1885. Between 1878 and 1882, the Auteuil studios, under the leadership of Felix Bracquemond, became the center of activity for Haviland art pottery in terra cotta, primarily vases and jardinieres. The decorations on the pieces were painted flat or appliqued with a soft paste and colored clays into a molded relief.

Examples of this form of artwork won prizes at the Philadelphia Exposition of 1876. The French artists, using the pottery as their canvas, gave a special quality to these vases with subtle glazing of color and artwork.

Charles Edward stopped producing pottery in 1882. It never became commercially successful as the art work was too impressionistic for the ordinary taste. There are no examples shown here.

Between 1882 and 1885, brown stoneware was manufactured by Haviland under the direction of Chaplet in the Vaugirard studio.

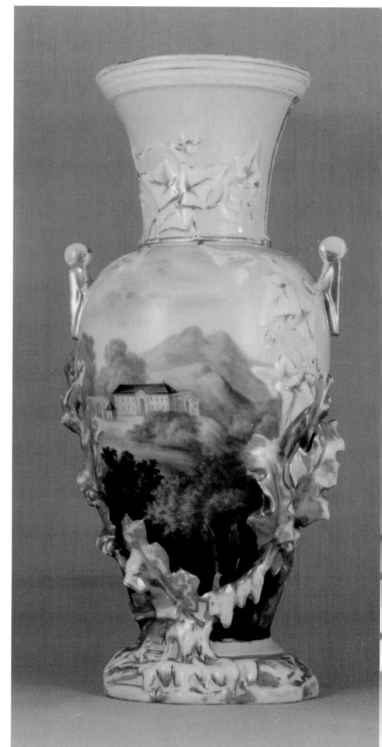

Figure 135. Porcelain vase, 15" tall, factory decorated. Haviland & Company, 1853, Mark A. *Courtesy of Marty Tackitt.* $1500-2500.

Figure 136. Stoneware vase, shows front scene, 15" high by 9"
wide. Different scene on back. Haviland and Company, 1876-
1889. There are four marks: Impression of H & Co., F, g, and
on side, written in gold, H & Co. *Courtesy of Marty Tackitt.*
$1500-2500.

Figure 137. Side view of stoneware vase in Fig. 136, showing girl's head in relief. Haviland and Company, 1876-1889. *Courtesy of Marty Tackitt.*

Figure 138. Stoneware jug, 12" high. Haviland & Company, 1876-1889, Marks F and g. *Courtesy of Marty Tackitt.* $900-1500.

Figure 139. Porcelain vase, 9" high by 9" wide and only 2¼" deep, with portrait of woman and Meadow Visitors. Hand painted and signed by factory artist Boilvin. Haviland & Company, 1876-1889, Marks D and g. $1200-1800.

Figure 140. Jardiniere, Charles Field Haviland, CFH/GDM, 1882-1891. *Courtesy of Marty Tackitt.* $800-1200.

Figure 141. Porcelain vase with handle, painted and signed by Felix Bracquemond. Haviland & Company, 1877, Mark E. *Courtesy of Marty Tackitt.* $1000-1400.

Figure 142. Celadon porcelain pitcher, 8" tall by 3" wide, factory decorated. Haviland & Company, 1877-1889, Marks E and g. *Courtesy of Marty Tackitt.* $250-350.

Presidential China

Haviland china was first used during the Lincoln Administration in 1861. These pieces are unmarked, as the china was purchased ten years before Haviland & Company started to mark their dinnerware; but the porcelain is of the same quality and molds of a Haviland set from a later date, and bear the decorator mark of E.V. Haughwout and Company. The first backmarks show up in 1877 in additional pieces of the Lincoln pattern ordered by President U.S. Grant, and again in 1884 with President Chester A. Arthur. This was a royal purple and gold dinner service, with the American eagle in the center.

In 1869, President Grant ordered a state dinner service with flowers in the center, a Coat of Arms, and a mustard-colored border. The Lincoln, Grant and Hayes sets were used as long as there remained sufficient numbers of pieces for a formal function. Mrs. Kennedy had a fondness for Grant's Coat of Arms set, but there was so little left by the 1960s that she was able to use it only for luncheons.

The most famous presidential dinnerware set was designed for the Rutherford B. Hayes administration by Theodore Davis, a former artist/writer for *Harper's Weekly*. Davis was an avid fisherman and hunter as well as a renowned artist of nature and wildlife. He came to the White House one day in 1879 to supervise photographing the President with his cabinet for an illustration. He met Mrs. Hayes in the Conservatory as she was trying to decide on a pattern with ferns for the new White House china. Davis suggested she showcase the American spirit in the dinner set; and Mrs. Hayes, enthusiastic about the idea, asked Theodore Davis to personally see to the design of the new set. This set consisted of flora and fauna, with pieces in various shapes, bold designs and vivid colors — all representing aspects of American wildlife.

Davis, a painter, photographer, and designer, knew nothing about the design traditions of dinnerware or the process of pattern making. He sent his watercolors with detailed color notations, which became both impossible and impractical economically to duplicate. These designs were so difficult to produce on porcelain that Haviland & Company was forced to invent new methods for production.

An original price had been agreed upon of $3,120.00, but because of the unusual designs for the dinnerware, the cost to manufacture far exceeded this price. The presidential seal was usually put on the front of each piece, but because the seal would look out of place on this unusual set, it was agreed that Haviland could place the seal on the back. The set was finally delivered to the White House in 1879 and had Theodore Davis' initials, signature and date inscribed on the back of each piece, along with the normal backstamp and the presidential seal.

Two complete sets were made: one for the White House; and the second with hopes of selling it to the Prince of Wales. The Prince did not like it and the set was eventually bought by the Governor General of Canada. The set caused a great sensation; everyone had an opinion, they either loved or hated it. Haviland duplicated some of the pieces from the service for general sale in an effort to recoup their enormous financial loss. Most of the pieces were probably bought because they were copies from the White House set, not because the public liked them. Some people, however, did like the novelty of parts of the service.

The Hayes set was first used by outgoing President and Mrs. Hayes for an intimate dinner for the newly elected President and Mrs. Garfield in November of 1880, and first used for a state function in honor of President and Mrs. Grant on their return from a world tour in December of the same year. For unabashed assertion of national pride, no china could outshine this exuberant dinner service. The White House Guide of 1973 mentions that according to one report at the state dinner, it became "the most conspicuous part of the furniture of the table." Presidents Arthur and Cleveland used it, and extra pieces to replace broken ones were purchased from J.W. Boteler and Son of Washington, D.C. These had the backstamp for the china sold on the open market as well as the patent mark.

The *Drop Rose* pattern with cobalt and gold trim was sold to Mrs. McKinley in 1900 for the McKinley's personal use. This backstamp showed "Dulin and Martin Company of Washington, D.C." on the back with the Haviland backstamp.

Pressure was on after 1900 to use only American-made china. The last Haviland china service used in the White House was a set of *Theodore Haviland, Made in America*. There are no definite records available, but it is thought that this set was purchased to use at the New York World's Fair. Luncheon was served to the King and Queen of England in the Federal Building at the fair on Saturday, June 10, 1939. The service plates and after-dinner coffee cups and saucers were made by Lenox.

Because of a special clause in the appropriation bills during the 19th century, "decayed furnishings" could be sold and the proceeds used to buy replacements. Several times over the years, the cupboards were swept clean and the china was carted off to auction. Much china, that was deemed too damaged to use, was simply given away.

In 1889, Mrs. Benjamin Harrison decided it was time to start collecting some of the pieces from the previous administrations. Mrs McKinley continued the project, with the collection greatly expanded through the efforts of Mrs. Theodore Roosevelt, who greatly opposed selling any of the White House china. In 1908, Mrs. Roosevelt asked that the damaged china be broken up and scattered in the Potomac River.

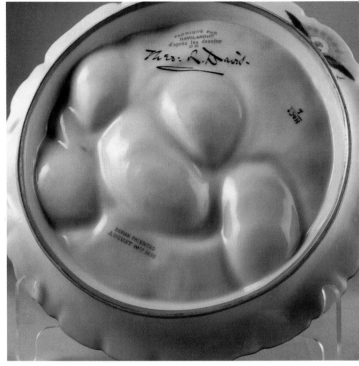

Figure 144. Back of oyster plate in Fig. 143, showing Eagle symbol, signature by artist Theodore Davis, and patented stamp showing date of August 10, 1880. *Courtesy of Marty Tackitt.*

Figure 145. Soup bowl, 9" diameter, from the President Rutherford B. Hayes White House service. Haviland & Company, 1880, signed by Theodore R. Davis, Mark F and also one similar to Mark a. *Courtesy of HCIF, Art Wendt Photographer.* $800-1200.

Figure 143. Oyster plate from the President Rutherford B. Hayes White House service, in cobalt and gold. Haviland & Company, 1880, Marks F and a. *Courtesy of Marty Tackitt.* $800-1200.

Part 3:
Dining with Haviland China

European Influence

France was considered the hub of civilization during the middle 1850s, and Haviland & Company enjoyed great patronage from the royal families. Empress Eugenie, wife of Napoleon III, was one of many who purchased large sets of Haviland china for dining — the more lavish the set the better. One of the princesses of France was rumored to have had 18 complete services for 48 people in her possession at one time!

During this period, Haviland created very elaborate sets with large serving pieces rimmed with heavy gold. Furnishings at this time were heavy, over-draped with layers of carpets and fabric, and the china was just as ostentatious.

Queen Victoria of England was fond of Haviland china. Her daughter, the Empress Fredricke of Germany, is said to have taken four services of Haviland with her upon her marriage, a substantial portion of which can still be found in a museum in Berlin. Haviland china could also be found at the Russian court; and, in fact, won an award in Moscow for excellence. Queen Mary of England was a great admirer of Haviland china and ordered a monogrammed service for her personal use.

Figure 146. Ornate early coffee pot, creamer and sugar bowl fashioned in the *Old Paris* style. Haviland & Company, 1853, Mark A. *Courtesy of Marty Tackitt.* 3 pieces $600-1500.

Figure 147. Same pattern as Fig. 146. Dinner plate, tea cup/saucer and slurp dish, all part of a complete dinner service. Tea or coffee was poured into the smaller dish, cooled and then drank. Haviland & Company, 1853, Mark A. *Courtesy of Marty Tackitt.* Pieces as shown $150-200.

Haviland Comes to America

Haviland & Company found that with the popularity of their porcelain in Europe, they had a great new market in the United States. David Haviland was quick to capitalize on the fact that Americans did not have a royal family to follow and that everything royal from Europe brought attention. The Expositions held in Europe and America were largely public attractions that really set the fashion trends in living. International displays told the public how their dining table was to look and which china was fashionable.

The southern states bought large sets of Haviland china in abundance, as the time before the Civil War was one of lavish parties. Those pre-Civil War years were also a time for wealthy Southerners to acquire the best of everything money could buy. After the Civil War, the ranks and fortunes of the extremely wealthy in the North had grown enormous. With large profits from industrial and commercial expansion, businessmen were wealthier by far than the wealthiest of the antebellum elite.

As the American new wealth grew with the Vanderbilts, Jay Goulds and other railroad and land barons, *they* became American royalty. The middle class family wanted to emulate the rich by trying to live a pared-down version of their lifestyles. Haviland & Company was intuitive enough to realize that they had a wide open market in the china business. The company created several patterns of economical Haviland china available through mail order catalogs. An average twelve place dinner service shown in the 1904 edition of the Sears, Roebuck and Company catalog (100 pieces shipped in a barrel) sold for $19.95. A service with more gold and elaborate design could retail for $39.95 or more. This brought Haviland dinnerware into the "Middle American" home during the turn of the twentieth century.

Shipments to the United States in 1900 numbered 18,000 barrels; and by 1906, they shipped over 28,000 in a single year. The years from 1893 to 1903 could probably be considered the *Golden Years* for Haviland & Company and Theodore Haviland Company. More china was shipped during that ten years than in any other period of Haviland history.

Dining Customs in the "Age of Elegance"

American cuisine, though abundant in quantity, was sadly lacking in elegance; so the Americans turned to Europe, particularly to the cuisine and dining manners of the French. Long before the American Civil War, French food had been considered the height of elegance and sophistication, and French chefs were in demand in the better hotels and wealthier homes. According to etiquette books of the 1880s, French manners were considered more graceful than the English.

To have some essence of social class, a person preferred to dine rather than just eat. The decade of the 1880s was considered the "Age of Excess" in which conspicuous consumption was a way to distinguish the upper class from those of a lower socioeconomic scale. Before the invention of television and radio, dining was the main source of entertainment and dinner parties were held on a grand scale as often as every night.

By 1880, New York City had become the model for elite manners and good taste. *Haute cuisine* at elaborate and expensive dinner parties became the way high society could separate themselves from the newly rich, such as Diamond Jim Brady and Lillian Russell. To the socially elite, only the very elegant person could appreciate the sophistication of French food.

Dining and etiquette habits varied from decade to decade. What was in vogue in 1870 would perhaps be out of style by 1880. The use of certain dishes and foods depended on which decade you were talking about. This book does not attempt to show every minute culture change, but scans an *era* of dining with Haviland china.

By the mid-1800s, the American mode of life was changing. With cities getting larger, men worked farther from home. This necessitated the development of public transportation and a drastic change in the family's schedule for their major meal away from midday; thus evening meals with the family or guests became larger and more leisurely.

Prior to the 1850s, most meals were served "family-style." Food was served by the course, but in large bowls or platters placed in the middle of the table. Guests helped themselves and then passed the food around the table. There would have been two or three tablecloths layered on the dining table, with a thicker dark cloth as the bottom layer if the table was scratched or damaged. As the tablecloths would get soiled easily with the food being passed and dished up, at the end of each course a servant would remove the used plates, serving dishes, silverware and one layer of tablecloth. By the end of the evening, dessert would be served on the shining wood top of the dining table.

From the 1850s on, serving *à la Russe* became fashionable. A butler would carve from the sideboard and arrange each plate for the servant to serve each guest. This method of serving cleared the table of excess china and allowed for large floral decorations to adorn the table. However most of these decorations were so large in size as to limit any discussion across the table. Visiting was limited to the left or the right. This also allowed for more silver and crystal pieces to be placed on the table.

With the arrival of *service à la Russe*, large bowls and platters that had been used in family-style dining were replaced with an astonishing array of silver, glassware, china and implements created to prepare, season and eat the variety of foods placed on the table. The amount of serving help had to be increased with this style of dining. More domestic staff was required for the polishing of silver and the washing of china, linen and crystal.

Special pantries were built to accommodate all of the items necessary for these dinner parties. Larger kitchens were built, inventions in cooking items developed, methods of refrigeration adapted and special washrooms were created just for the *good china*. Thin copper basins were used for this purpose as the china was less apt to chip against the soft side of the copper. These basins were placed in the same room where the china was stored. A family might have several services of Haviland china, containing as many place settings as their dining room could accommodate. There would be very fine sets with gold trim for dinner, plus the more simple sets for breakfast and luncheon.

Middle class America watched the wealthy upper class entertain and wanted to partake in this show of elegance and prosperity. The average American woman had at least one serving girl to help her with meals or could hire one for a special evening. Courses were not quite as lavish or numerous, but she could still serve at least three or four. As time passed, these meals became more formal. Engraved invitations were sent to the guests, and place cards and menus arranged on the table.

By 1880, a modified *service à la Russe* was popular among the middle class. A serving girl would serve the side dishes from a sideboard, with the host carving the main meat at the table. The elaborate sideboard, a sign of prestige, was to become one of the most expensive items purchased in the average home. By 1885, dining had become so formal in the average household, some guests were moaning the loss of comfort and hospitality. This new style of entertaining seemed to be more concerned with impressing the guest with the beautiful china, silver and crystal than making the guest comfortable.

The sheer volume of food served at meals was overwhelming, but there is every indication that most of it was consumed. Large amounts of heavy, rich food were eaten as none of the foods served were created to be *low fat*. Photos of men dining in the 1800s would show many of them very robust, flaunting their weight with gold watch chains and jeweled stickpins shining. Victorian women were expected to show more restraint in dining, although plumpness was regarded as a sign of good health; and starchy foods, fats and sweets were recommended by health experts!

With the advent of World War I, things began to change. Men went overseas and women took their places in the offices and stores. Servants were difficult to acquire as there was more money to be made in an office or shop, and the work was not so physically taxing. By the mid-1920s, women wanted to dance and play; they were no longer interested in sitting in a dining room and eating large meals. Being healthy and thin were in, styles were no longer corseted and, therefore, heavy meals were not in vogue.

Haviland eliminated several of the place setting pieces and many of the extra serving pieces needed to serve a complete meal in the 1870s to the 1890s. Gone were the individual butter dishes, bone dishes, oyster plates, artichoke plates, fish and game sets, etc. Most of the sets made in the 1920s consisted of just dinner, luncheon, salad, bread and butter plates, tea or coffee cups and saucers, plus five or six serving pieces. Today, many of the sets are also dishwasher proof.

Breakfast

Breakfast was almost as elaborate as dinner. Americans wanted something more substantial than breads and coffee, and kept to their meats, omelettes, potatoes, etc. By the 1880s, the morning meal had become a special event among the upper class. Breakfast was often pushed into mid-morning because of late risers, creating more of a brunch. Guests were entertained, especially in large summer homes, and fed massive amounts of food. The breakfast table would be set with flowers, Haviland china, silver and glassware, but in a more informal way. The more expensive Haviland china would be reserved for dinner.

There was a love of completeness during this time, especially in the realm of dinnerware. Every woman wanted as complete a set of Haviland as she could possibly afford. This included special pieces for every meal served throughout the day. Haviland & Company and other porcelain manufacturers started creating breakfast services that corresponded to their popular patterns, but with larger coffee cups and smaller plates. With the advent of packaged ready-to-eat breakfast cereal in the 1870s, cereal bowls were supplied.

Bread and butter plates were used for either toast and jam at breakfast or at supper with soup and bread. There was a period in the 1880s and 1890s when it was frowned upon to serve bread and butter at formal dinners, as some found it repugnant to see someone spreading butter on a piece of bread, holding and eating it with their hands and fingers. This is written in several of the etiquette books of that time period. Perhaps they saw the intimacy of it as a breakfast occupation. Bread and butter was served sometimes exclusively at tea but then bite-sized pieces of bread were already buttered.

Haviland created many pieces to grace the morning meal; the jam jar, cereal bowls, egg cups in various sizes and shapes, pancake and muffin servers, plus any other serving dish that related to breakfast food.

Mary Jewry, in an 1890s edition of *Warne's Model Cookery*, stated that a lady's taste and refinement were very perceptible at the breakfast table. A nicely laid, pretty, appetizing breakfast was a great promoter of good temper and harmony through the ensuing day. Miss Jewry wrote:

"Let our homes ever be bright, sunny, and charming; and that such may be the case open the day with a cheery and well-arranged breakfast-table."

Figure 148. Breakfast set: cereal bowl with underplate and milk pitcher, in Schleiger no. 1303. Charles Field Haviland, CFH/GDM, 1882-1890. Set $100-175.

Figure 149. Cereal bowl in unidentified pattern on Ranson blank with gold Schleiger no. 24 trim. Note the pattern covers the outside as well as inside. Haviland & Company, 1894-1931, Marks I and c. $25-40.

Figure 150. Rimmed oatmeal bowl in Schleiger no. 272. Haviland & Company, 1894-1931, Marks I and c. $25-40.

Figure 151. Buckwheat pancake server in unidentified pattern. Charles Field Haviland, CFH/GDA, after 1900. *Courtesy of Marty Tackitt.* $165-250.

Figure 152. Covered muffin server in Schleiger no. 72. Dome of muffin server is slightly higher than a pancake server. Haviland & Company, 1894-1931, Marks I and c. *Courtesy of Marty Tackitt.* $165-250.

Figure 153. Egg tray in Schleiger no. 257, Ranson blank on gold no. 24. Haviland & Company, 1888-1896, Marks H and c. *Courtesy of Marty Tackitt.* $175-275.

Figure 154. Honey dish, 4" in diameter and flat, in Schleiger no. 22. Haviland & Company, 1900-1931, Marks I and c. $25-35.

Figure 156. Individual syrup pitcher, 3½", in unidentified pattern. Theodore Haviland, 1903, Mark q. $75-125.

Figure 155. Syrup pitcher with underplate in Schleiger no. 20A. The lid has a deep rim that fits down inside the pot with cutout at pouring spout. A chocolate pot would have a regular lid with inside small tab to keep lid from falling when pouring. Haviland & Company, 1894-1931, Marks I and c. *Courtesy of Marty Tackitt.* $125-225.

Figure 157. Marmalade or jam jar, underplate missing, in Schleiger no. 877. This jar has no hole in bottom. Jam was placed directly into jar, with an opening in lid to place a silver jam spoon. Theodore Haviland, 1903, Mark p. $125-225.

Figure 158. 3 piece jam jar in Christmas Rose pattern (popular name, not in Schleiger books). This jar has hole in bottom to allow a canned jar of jam to be placed inside and later removed. Breakfast tables were set with fine Haviland and it would be unseemly to place a plain glass jar on the table. Haviland & Company, 1894-1903, Marks I and c. $225-325.

Figure 159. Egg cups, *left to right*: Schleiger no. 57H, Blank no. 20, & Schleiger no. 904. The middle egg cup is a single egg cup; the outer cups, called American egg cups, were used for a single or double egg as shown. Haviland & Company, 1894-1931, Marks I and c. Left to right: Single cup $35-65. American cup $55-75.

Figure 160. Footed egg cup in unidentified pattern on blank no. 205. Haviland & Company, 1894-1931, Marks I and c. $65-95.

Figure 161. Footed egg cup in *Baltimore Rose*, Schleiger no. 1151B. Haviland & Company, 1894-1931, Marks I and c. *Courtesy of Marty Tackitt.* $75-150.

Figure 162. Footed egg cup in unidentified pattern on Marseille blank. Haviland & Company, 1888-1896, Marks H and i. $65-95.

Figure 163. *Baltimore Rose* Café au Lait cup and saucer, Schleiger no. 1151B. These cups were popular in the South. Cake and donuts were dunked in coffee; the bottom of the cup would contain the rich cake and coffee mixture, which was then eaten with a spoon. This is a large cup, larger than a coffee cup. Haviland & Company, 1894-1931, Marks I and c. $95-175.

Figure 164. Chocolate set with 4 chocolate cups and saucers in Schleiger no. 780 on smooth blank. Haviland & Company, 1894-1931, Marks I and c. $395-600.

Luncheon

Luncheon as an occasion for entertaining was first introduced in the 1850s. This became a feminine pastime as most of the men were too busy at their offices to return home during the day. The ladies found that this was the perfect opportunity to show hospitality with little expense to those whom they could not invite to dinner.

A woman entertaining her friends might possibly create the elegance of a small dinner party. Several courses would be offered; creamed oysters, lobster salads, cold chicken, roast beef, fruits, cakes, dozens of different sandwiches and desserts. Soup and fish were generally omitted during luncheon.

Smaller portions were served, therefore most of the plates, and serving bowls were downsized. There was a bowl or plate for every special item; especially several sizes and shapes of relish dishes as pickling was very popular: tomatoes, apples, cucumbers, nasturtiums, eggs, onions, etc. All were pickled and each needed its own special bowl, comport or dish.

A number of various vegetable and fruit jellies were served along with preserves and relishes — cranberry sauce and mint jelly are but a few. Certain meat dishes were always accompanied by various jellies, for luncheon as well as dinner parties.

Figure 165. Olive dish in Baltimore Rose on Schleiger no. 19. Haviland & Company, 1894-1931, Marks I and c. *Courtesy of Marty Tackitt.* $75-125.

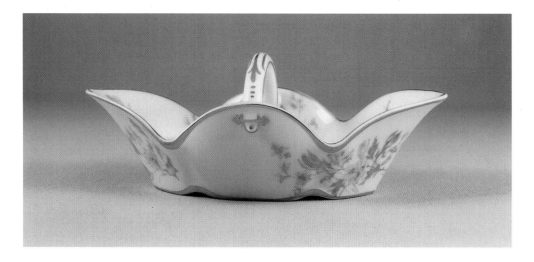

Figure 166. Olive dish with handle, unidentified pattern on Schleiger no. 19. Haviland & Company, 1894-1931, Marks I and c. *Courtesy of Marty Tackitt.* $95-150.

Figure 167. Small handled basket in Marseille Shape, Schleiger no. 9. Haviland & Company, 1876-1889, Mark F. *Courtesy of Marty Tackitt.* $95-145.

Figure 170. Fancy pickle dish in Marseille blank, Schleiger no. 9. Haviland & Company, 1877, Mark E. *Courtesy of Marty Tackitt.* $65-95.

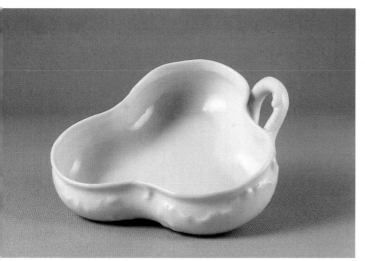

Figure 168. *Porte Olive Tricorne,* 3 cornered olive dish in Schleiger blank no. 122. Theodore Haviland, 1894, mark is combination of k and l in circle. $75-125.

Figure 169. Relish dish in Schleiger no. 235E. Haviland & Company, 1894-1931, Marks I and c. $45-65.

Figure 171. Ice relish, 8", in variation of Schleiger no. 1159 on blank no. 2. Haviland & Company, 1894-1931, Marks I and c. $75-95.

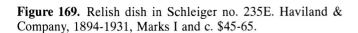

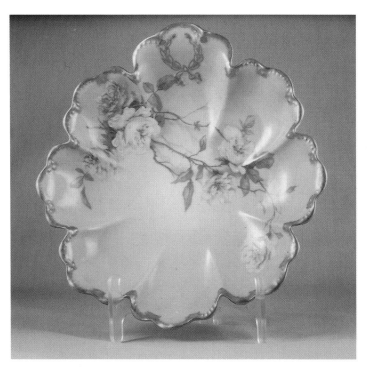

Figure 172. Ice relish, 8", in Baltimore Rose, pink background with white roses, blank no. 22. Haviland & Company, 1894-1931, Marks I and c. *Courtesy of Marty Tackitt.* $125-225.

Figure 173. Ice relish, 8", in Schleiger no. 65B. Haviland & Company, 1894-1931, Marks I and c. $75-95.

Figure 174. Individual lobster salad bowl, 7", in Schleiger no. 66N. Haviland & Company, 1894-1931, Marks I and c. $65-95.

Figure 175. Serving bowl with basket weave rim. Haviland & Company, 1888-1896, Marks H and c. *Courtesy of Marty Tackitt.* $225-400.

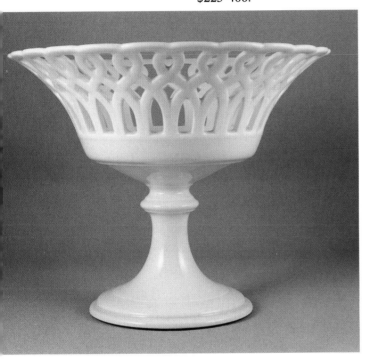

Figure 176. Tall footed comport in the basket weave form. Haviland & Company, 1876-1889, Mark F. $150-250.

Figure 177. Luncheon plate with cutouts in unidentified pattern on Marseille blank with gold trim. Haviland & Company, 1894-1931, Marks I and c. *Courtesy of Marty Tackitt.* $125-175.

Figure 178. Luncheon plate, 8½", in Schleiger no. 742A. Haviland & Company, 1894-1931, Marks I and c. $25-35.

Figure 180. Lemonade pitcher in Schleiger no. 475F. Haviland & Company, 1894-1931, Marks I and c. $195-275.

Figure 179. Large water or milk pitcher in Schleiger no. 34 on blank 12, 7 5/8" high. This is the second to the largest in this blank. Haviland did not make a large pitcher in Ranson blank and used this one with Ranson sets. Haviland & Company, 1894-1931, Marks I and c. $225-325.

Afternoon Tea

Luncheon was at first served at 1:30 or 2:00; then as breakfasts became lighter, luncheon was served earlier, 12:00 or 1:00. Since dinner wasn't usually served until somewhere between 7:30 and 9:00, there left a large uncomfortable gap between luncheon and dinner; hence by 1850, a small meal of tea and cakes became fashionable in all the fine houses.

Tea was usually served at 5:00 and could be a very simple repast of thin sandwiches and cakes. *High teas* were mostly served on Sundays and consisted of dishes such as scalloped oysters, partridge, cold ham, an array of small cakes, sandwiches and at least one large cake.

As the serving of tea became more popular, hostesses would try to outdo each other with elaborate displays of their finest tea services, cake stands and table linens. Tea was an expensive commodity, and tea leaves were kept in very special containers, small carved chests made of fine wood or beautiful porcelain tea caddies. Specially shaped plates, sandwich trays, biscuit or cracker jars, comports of all sizes, bonbon trays and cake plates were all designed and became popular because of the custom of afternoon tea.

Figure 181. Eight cup tea pot with trivet in Schleiger no. 920. Haviland & Company, 1894-1931, Marks I and c. Pot $225-350, Trivet $65-95.

Figure 182. Trivet for round teapot with drip plate, hand painted gold trim. Haviland & Company, 1888-1896, Mark H. $145-225.

Figure 183. Tea caddy in Schleiger no. 1166 on Ranson blank. Haviland & Company, 1888-1896, Marks H and c. *Courtesy of Marty Tackitt.* $175-250.

Figure 185. Tea caddy in Schleiger no. 86A. Haviland & Company, 1888-1896, Mark H. $225-350.

Figure 184. Tea caddy in a variation of Schleiger no. 1150 on Blank no. 15. Haviland & Company, 1894-1931, Marks I and c. *Courtesy of Marty Tackitt.* $175-250.

Figure 186. Waste bowl in Schleiger no. 226A. This bowl was for the dregs of tea and lemon, etc. Haviland & Company, 1894-1931, Marks I and c. *Courtesy of Marty Tackitt.* $45-65.

Figure 187. Creamer and open sugar bowl in a variation of Schleiger no. 260, with forest green and gold trim and a large rose in center of sugar bowl. Haviland & Company, 1894-1903, Marks I and c. $125-225.

Figure 188. Sandwich tray set in unidentified pattern on Ranson blank with gold trim. Tea cup is smaller than regular tea cup to fit cup ring. Haviland & Company, 1888-1889, Marks H and c. *Courtesy of Marty Tackitt.* $125-165.

Figure 189. Sandwich tray set in unidentified pattern on Marseille blank. Haviland & Company, 1888-1896, Marks H and c. *Courtesy of Marty Tackitt.* $150-250.

Figure 190. Tea cup and saucer in Schleiger no. 480. Haviland & Company, 1876-1889, Marks F and c. $40-50.

Figure 191. Heart shaped plate (listed by this name in the 1889 Haviland Catalog, some people refer to this as the palette shape), 7", Marseille Schleiger no. 9. This plate came in four sizes and used for desserts or teas. Haviland & Company, 1876-1889, Mark F. $45-75.

Figure 192. Biscuit or Cracker jar in Schleiger no. 148A. Theodore Haviland, 1903, Mark p. $165-225.

Figure 193. Biscuit or Cracker jar in Schleiger no. 251 on Ranson blank. Haviland & Company, 1894-1931, Marks I and c. $175-275.

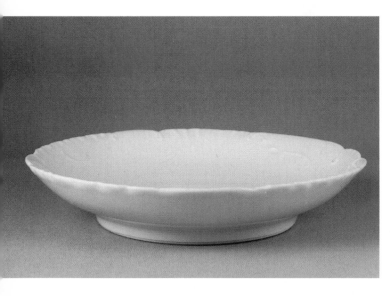

Figure 194. Round English comport in Marseille Shape, Schleiger no. 9. (Please note correct designation—compote is the fruit that fills the comport) Haviland & Company, 1888-1896, Mark H. $125-175.

Figure 195. Tall comport in Schleiger no. 146. Theodore Haviland, 1903, Mark p. $195-295.

Figure 196. English comport in Schleiger no. 257C. Haviland & Company, 1894-1931, Marks I and c. $125-225.

Figure 197. 3 compartment bonbon tray in Schleiger no. 53, with border of no. 524 on blank no. 10 with gold. Haviland & Company, 1910-1931, Mark I and special decorator mark of Frank Haviland, Paris, Limoges, France. $250-350.

Figure 199. Square cake plate in Schleiger no. 320B. Theodore Haviland, 1903, Mark q. $95-145.

Figure 198. Cake plate with open handles in Schleiger no. 248B on Ranson blank. Haviland & Company, 1894-1931, Marks I and c. $85-125.

Dinner Parties

By the late 1800s, dinner was considered the most important of all social occasions. A style of etiquette emerged as dinner parties became more elaborate with time. A wealthy society matron might give a dinner party once or twice a week, while a middle class woman might give just one a month if her budget allowed.

Dining was entertainment. It was not fashionable to be late to a dinner party. Guests arrived 15 minutes before the invitation stated, gathered and were then escorted to the table when dinner was announced as cocktail parties were unheard of during this period. There might have been as many as four or five dinner parties a week, with each one lasting up to four hours. A dinner party was given as a sign of social status as well as entertainment. Each dinner served was more grand than the last, *elegance* being the operative word. With each additional course that were served, the lady of the house was allowed to use and display more of her elegant china and serving pieces, thus telling everyone how wealthy she was.

With all of this dining among the upper and middle classes in America, we can see why Haviland flourished during these years. There was a large market for fine china in America and Haviland & Company was right in the middle of it. Elaborate sets with lots of gold trim were sold as well as very simple sets. As breakfast, luncheon, afternoon tea and dinner were important to the social life of upper and middle America, every family wanted to have that special set of Haviland china.

There could have been as many as 15 courses for dinner with usually a menu placed in front of each guest. This allowed the guest to make a choice of soups, entrees, desserts, etc. There also could be 10 to 15 pieces of silverware at each place setting along with glassware for various wines served throughout the meal. One study in the Haviland *Ranson* pattern found 65 pieces per place setting, and there are sure to be that many in other patterns. The well-appointed table would have all of the items for a comfortable meal within easy reach, so that one would not be required to ask or wait for anything, including: individual salt cellars, bone dishes, individual bean or vegetable bowls, etc. Bread and butter plates were not used at a dinner party as the roll was placed directly on the table or nestled in the napkin.

Many pieces of china were used in the various courses of a dinner party; only the wealthy would have been able to serve as many courses as listed below, plus the types of courses would vary as food preferences changed over the years. Several pieces were used for multiple purposes, even though they are represented here in only one course. Serving pieces through certain usage have been given names, such as a mashed potato dish or a noodle dish; but the original catalogs list quite a few of the bowls just by size.

The First Course: Oysters

Almost every meal began with raw oysters. These were considered to be the closest thing to a classless food because of their abundance and popularity. There were plates for three to six oysters with a place in the center for a sauce. Some plates were simple, others very unusual and costly.

Figure 200. Oyster plate in cobalt and gold. Haviland & Company, 1876-1889, Mark F. *Courtesy of Marty Tackitt.* $175-225.

Figure 201. Oyster plate in unidentified pattern. Haviland &
Company, 1894-1931, Marks I and c. $125-150.

Figure 202. Oyster plate in Schleiger no. 213. Haviland & Company, 1894-1931, Marks I and c. $125-150.

Figure 203. Oyster plate in Ranson blank, Schleiger no. 1.
Haviland & Company, 1894-1931, Mark I. $125-150.

Figure 204. Unusual oyster plate with raised leaves in gold. Theodore Haviland, 1893, Mark L. $145-175.

Figure 205. Oyster plate in Schleiger no. 73B. Haviland & Company, 1888-1896, Marks H and c. $125-150.

Figure 206. Rare petite oyster plate for three oysters. Charles Field Haviland, CFH/GDM mark with donut stamp, 1882-1890. $145-175.

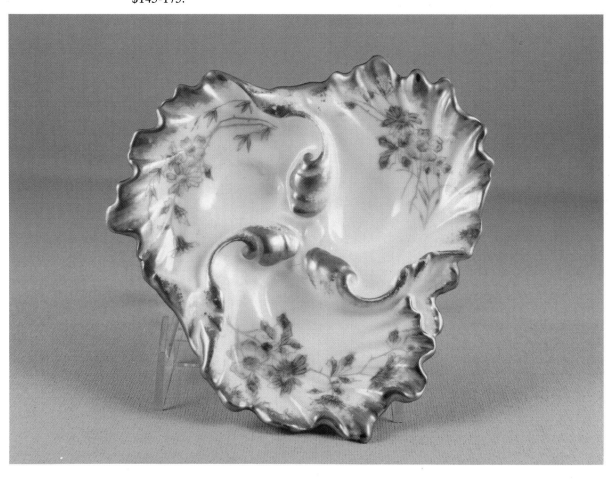

The Second Course: Soup

Soup or stew was an important part of dinner. There would have been both clear and thick soups offered at a dinner party. In low or middle class families, soup with bread might have been served as the evening meal, with the main meal being at noon. There were tureens for oyster stew, clam chowder and regular soups.

Soup bowls were designed for the correct soups. Clear broths were served in bouillon cups and were the same size and shape as tea cups but with two handles. Some of the bouillon cups came with covers to keep the soup warm until it was eaten. There were also cream soup bowls with underplates, rimmed soup bowls that came as a set with the soup tureens and coupe (rimless) soup bowls that came with the dinner service. There is also a 9" round bowl of the same depth as the regular soup bowl which may have been used for chowder or stew.

By the mid- to late 1800s, handles were for looks only — etiquette did not allow the bouillon and cream soup bowls to be picked up. Silver bouillon spoons were provided, as well as specialized spoons for every other type of soup.

There is no example of a porcelain soup ladle made by Haviland & Company in any of the old catalogs. Silver ladles, considered preferable, were more durable and elegant.

Figure 207. Oyster tureen, factory decorated in unidentified pattern, shape of Henri II, Schleiger no. 10. Haviland & Company, 1876-1883, Marks F and d. *Courtesy of Marty Tackitt.* $350-450.

Figure 208. Chowder tureen in napkin fold blank, Schleiger no. 1118. Haviland & Company, 1876, Mark F. $250-300.

Figure 209. Soup tureen in Schleiger no. 1047. Theodore Haviland, 1903, Mark p. $275-350.

Figure 210. Soup tureen in Schleiger no. 266B on Marseille blank. Haviland & Company, 1876-1889, Marks F and c. $250-325.

Figure 211. Soup tureen in unidentified pattern on Ranson blank with bow handles. Haviland & Company, 1894-1931, Marks I and c. $225-325.

Figure 212. Bouillon cup in Schleiger no. 31 on ruffled Ranson blank, sides are almost transparent. Haviland & Company, 1894-1931, Marks I and c. (with saucer) $45-65.

Figure 215. Covered bouillon cup and saucer in unusual pink and gold design. Haviland & Company, 1888-1896, Marks H and c. *Courtesy of Marty Tackitt.* $85-125.

Figure 213. Bouillon cup and saucer in Schleiger no. 248B. Haviland & Company, 1894-1931, Marks I and c. $45-50.

Figure 216. Covered bouillon cup and saucer in variation of Amstel, Schleiger no. 497, on smooth blank. Haviland & Company, 1894-1931, Marks I and c. $65-85.

Figure 214. *Baltimore Rose* bouillon cup and saucer on pedestal, smooth blank shape with unidentified gold trim. Haviland & Company, 1894-1931, Marks I and c. $65-85.

Figure 217. Covered bouillon cup and saucer in unusual shape. Charles Field Haviland, 1882-1890, Mark CFH/GDM with donut. *Courtesy of R & J Mairs.* $75-125.

Figure 218. Covered broth bowl with underplate in Schleiger no. 1139. Haviland & Company, 1894-1931, Marks I and c. $95-150.

Figure 219. Cream soup bowl and underplate in Schleiger no. 890. Theodore Haviland, 1894-1903, Marks M and p. $45-65.

Figure 220. Coupe soup bowl in blush decorated finish. Haviland & Company, 1876-1889, Marks F and g. $35-45.

Figure 221. Rimmed soup bowl in Schleiger no. 145. Theodore Haviland, 1895, Mark n. $30-50.

Figure 222. 9" shallow serving bowl in *Countess*, Schleiger no. 69. May have been used for chowder or stew. Haviland & Company, 1894-1931, Marks I and c. $45-65.

The Third Course: Hors d'oeuvres

Anchovies, sardines, pickled oysters, cucumbers or celery might have been served at this course. Any type of fancy tray or platter would have been used.

Figure 223. Celery dish in Schleiger no. 1134 on blank no. 19. Haviland & Company, 1894-1931, Marks I and c. $95-125.

Figure 224. Celery dish, unidentified pattern on Ranson blank with gold trim. Haviland & Company, 1894-1931, Marks I and c. $125-145.

Figure 225. Bread tray in unidentified blank and pattern. Haviland & Company, Marks I and c. *Courtesy of Marty Tackitt.* $145-195.

Figure 226. Bread tray in Schleiger no. 434, 15". Haviland & Company, 1894-1931, Marks I and c. $125-165.

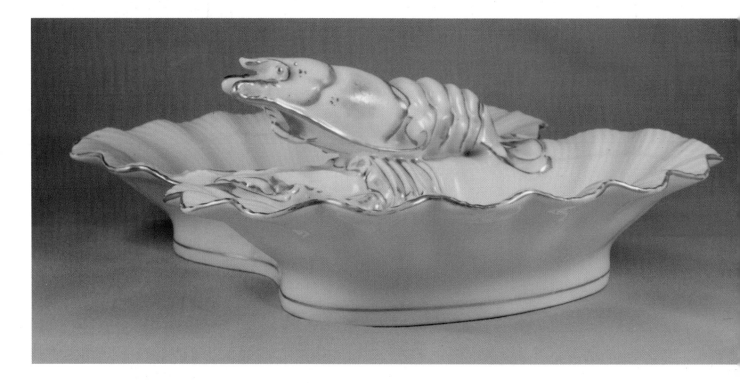

Figure 227. Lobster two-shelled comport, factory decorated in gold. Haviland & Company, 1876-1889, Marks F and g. $250-375.

Figure 228. Pickle or olive dish in Schleiger no. 42G. Haviland & Company, 1894-1931, Mark I plus unusual import backstamp. $45-65.

Figure 229. Backstamp of Olive dish in Fig. 228 reads *"Fine China, Pool, Importer Jobber."*

The Fourth Course:
Fresh Fish

Fish of almost any kind was used, from cod to a whole salmon. Fish was poached, fried, steamed, and served with or without sauce. The platters were over 22" long to allow for very large fish. Fish sets frequently had pictures of marine life painted on them, with a different scene on each plate. Sets hand painted by factory artists are highly valued by collectors.

Figure 230. *Feu de Four* fish platter with cobalt and gold trim, part of a set. Haviland & Company, 1893-1895, Marks H & h. *Courtesy of Marty Tackitt.* Complete set $3500-4500.

Figure 231. *Feu de Four* sauce boat for fish platter in Fig. 230. *Courtesy of Marty Tackitt.*

Figure 232. *Feu de Four* plate from fish set in Fig. 230, one of twelve. *Courtesy of Marty Tackitt.*

Figure 233. *Feu de Four* plate from fish set in Fig. 230, one of twelve. *Courtesy of Marty Tackitt.*

Figure 234. One of a set of fish plates. Charles Field Haviland, 1882-1890, CFH/GDM. $145-200.

Figure 235. Fish platter in Marseille, 22", Schleiger no. 9 with brown, fading to creme; gold trim in center has small fish within the pattern. Part of a set, Haviland & Company, 1888-1896, Marks H & c. Complete set $2500-3000.

Figure 236. Fish plate, sauce boat and serving bowl from fish set described in Fig. 235. There are twelve plates in set.

The Fifth Course:
Relevés (or Removes)

This course might have consisted of a substantial joint of roast beef, lamb or braise of meat, served with two or three green vegetables and potatoes. Haviland created special meat platters, as well as individual meat plates. Most of the meat dishes would have a sauce on the side. As refrigeration was lacking in the early years, sauce was sometimes used to mask the flavor of the meat. Most of the sauce boats are shown in this section, but they were used with other courses as well. There is only one example of a gravy ladle in Marseille blank in the old catalogs.

Bone dishes might be used during this course and also during the fish or game course if a special fish or game set was not used (Haviland did not make bone dishes to match the game sets).

Figure 237. Individual beef plate, 9½", in *Baltimore Rose*, Schleiger no. 1151B. Indentations and well in plate hold beef juice or gravy. Haviland & Company, 1894-1931, Marks I and c. *Courtesy of Marty Tackitt.* $200-250.

Figure 238. Sauce boat, 6½", with underplate in variation of Schleiger no. 921. Haviland & Company, 1894-1931, Marks I and c. $95-125.

Figure 239. Gravy boat with attached underplate in Schleiger no. 255 on Ranson blank in twig style. Haviland made two different styles of Ranson — twig handles and bow handles. The twig style has more ruffles and sits lower to table. Original sketches show patent date of 1895 for this blank. Haviland & Company, 1894-1931, Marks I and c. $95-125.

Figure 240. Gravy boat with attached underplate in Schleiger no. 46 on Ranson blank in bow style. Bow style sits up on ruffled foot and is smoother in shape. This blank shows patent date of 1893. Haviland & Company, 1893-1931, Marks I and c. $95-125.

Figure 241. Oval covered sauce tureen with attached underplate. The undercoloring is called a blush finish, put on with the first firing, finished and decorated in the normal fashion. Haviland & Company, 1876-1889, Marks F and g. $150-175.

Figure 242. Covered sauce tureen with attached underplate in unidentified pattern on Ranson blank with bow top. Haviland & Company, 1894-1931, Marks I and c. $125-145.

Figure 243. Covered sauce tureen with attached underplate in Schleiger no. 266 on the Marseille blank. Haviland & Company, 1876-1889, Marks F and c. $125-145.

Figure 244. Handled sauce boat with attached underplate, unidentified pattern. Haviland & Company, 1876-1889, Mark F and also backmark showing Decorated by Ovington Bros. $145-175.

Figure 245. Bone dishes, *left* Theodore Haviland, Schleiger no. 150, 1903, Mark p. *Right*, Haviland & Company, Schleiger no. 87, 1894-1931, Marks I and c. $20-25 each.

Figure 246. Bone dish, crescent shape in Schleiger no. 73, Haviland & Company, 1876-1889, Marks F and c. $20-25.

Figure 247. Oval bone dish in the Marseille shape, Schleiger no. 9. Haviland & Company, Mark F. $20-25.

The Sixth Course:
Sorbet

This was also called *Roman Punch,* a lemon sorbet often spiked with rum or champagne and served for a refreshing interlude after the rich salmon and duck courses to cleanse the palate.

In Europe, and presumably in America, certain jellies were served between courses instead of sorbet.

Figure 248. Sorbet or Sherbet dish in Schleiger no. 276. Haviland & Company, 1894-1931, Marks I and c. $65-75.

Figure 249. Sorbet or Sherbet dish with attached underplate in Schleiger no. 855A. Theodore Haviland, 1903, Mark p. $75-125.

The Seventh Course: The Entree

This course consisted of croquettes, sweet breads, fricassees, etc. garnished with vegetables, either on the same plate or in individual vegetable dishes. Some vegetables might be served with sauce, in special gelatin molds or on their own special Haviland plates. Asparagus with Hollandaise sauce was a popular vegetable served.

Figure 250. 12" platter in Schleiger no. 78B. Haviland & Company, 1894-1931, Marks I and c. $75-85.

Figure 251. Asparagus plate in Marseille shape, Schleiger no. 9, unidentified pattern. Asparagus spears are molded into plate at bottom side of dish. Hollandaise sauce was placed into small round section. Haviland & Company, 1888-1896, Marks H & c. *Courtesy of Marty Tackitt.* $200-250.

Figure 252. Individual vegetable bowl, sometimes called a "beaner," in Schleiger no. 133. Theodore Haviland, 1903, Mark p. $65-85.

Figure 253. Round handled serving bowl in Schleiger no. 442D. Haviland & Company, 1894-1931, Marks I and c. $85-100.

Figure 254. Round handled serving bowl in Schleiger no. 57A. Haviland & Company, 1894-1931, Marks I and c. $85-100.

Figure 256. Unusual serving bowl with one handle but no pouring spout. An early catalog shows a spooner in the same size and with three feet such as this one, but without a handle. Theodore Haviland, unidentified pattern, 1903, Mark p. $95-125.

Figure 255. Round covered casserole in Schleiger no. 523. Haviland & Company, 1894-1931, Marks I and c. $95-135.

The Eighth Course:
Venison, Wild Pigeon or Other Game.

This was sometimes referred to as the *Roast* course, usually canvas-back ducks and quail. However, since hunting was considered great sport, any other wild game might be used. As with the fish sets, most of the game plates had wild birds or game of some kind factory painted in the center of the platter and the plates.

Figure 257. Game bird platter in cobalt and gold. Theodore Haviland, 1903, Mark q. *Courtesy of Marty Tackitt.* Complete set $3200-3500.

Figure 258. Game bird plate, one of twelve, with platter shown in Fig. 257. *Courtesy of Marty Tackitt.*

Figure 259. Game bird plate, one of twelve, with platter shown in Fig. 257. *Courtesy of Marty Tackitt.*

Figure 260. Game bird plate on Osier blank no. 211 with gold trim. This and next three plates are from a set, all with a different scene. Haviland & Company, 1876-1889, Marks F and g. $125-175 ea.

Figure 262. Game bird plate.

Figure 261. Game bird plate on Osier blank no. 211 with gold trim. Haviland & Company, 1876-1889, Marks F and g.

Figure 263. Game bird plate.

Figure 264. Small game bird plate with cobalt and gold trim. Charles Field Haviland, 1882-1890, CFH/GDM with Ovington Bros. in gold crescent. $125-150.

Figure 265. Game bird plate on Ranson blank with floral border, cobalt and gold trim. Haviland & Company, 1888-1896, Marks H and c. *Courtesy of Marty Tackitt.* $150-195.

Figure 266. Game bird plate with Meadow Visitor border. Haviland & Company, 1876-1889, Marks D and g. *Courtesy of Marty Tackitt.* $175-225.

Figure 267. Game bird plate on napkin fold, embossed plate. Each plate in set has different animal, this one has bears. Haviland & Company, 1876-1889, Marks F and g. *Courtesy of Marty Tackitt.* $175-225.

Figure 268. Large 16" oval platter from game bird set in Torse blank, Schleiger no. 413 with pink trim. Haviland & Company, 1876-1886, Marks D and g. Complete set $2000-2500.

Figure 269. Game bird plate from set in Fig. 268. Haviland & Company, 1876-1886, Marks D and g.

Figure 271. Game bird plate from set in Fig. 268. Haviland & Company, 1876-1886, Marks D and g.

Figure 270. Game bird plate from set in Fig. 268. Haviland & Company, 1876-1886, Marks D and g.

Figure 272. Game bird plate from set in Fig. 268. Haviland & Company, 1876-1886, Marks D and g.

The Ninth Course: Salad

Today, we think of salad as being mainly green lettuce. In the late 1800s, however, salad was a little bit of everything. Greens were usually available only in spring or summer, and then primarily in the country. Salads were made from various vegetables, beans, beets, turnip tops, as well as macaroni and potatoes. One popular dish, *lobster salad*, was included at almost every dinner party. Haviland made several styles of salad bowls, in every pattern and shape. Here are but a few.

Figure 273. Salad plate in variation of Schleiger no. 1190. Plate measures 4½" x 9" and is in the shape of a bean. Bean stem curls into plate. Haviland & Company, 1887-1889, Marks G and g. $75-95.

Figure 274. Large salad bowl in Cannelé shape, unidentified pattern. Haviland & Company, 1888-1896, Marks H & c. $275-350.

Figure 275. Salad bowl in unidentified pattern in Richelieu blank. Haviland & Company, 1876-1889, Marks F and c. *Courtesy of Marty Tackitt.* $275-350.

Figure 276. Large salad bowl in *Drop Rose* pattern, Schleiger no. 55C. Haviland & Company, 1894-1931, Marks I and c. *Courtesy of R & J Mairs.* $450-750.

Figure 277. Master lobster salad bowl in variation of Schleiger no. 667. Lobster tail shells were inverted, placed in each rounded edge, and lobster salad was placed in center. Haviland & Company, 1888-1896, Marks H and c. $225-325.

Figure 278. Large salad bowl in Schleiger no. 609E. Theodore Haviland, 1903, Mark p. $225-250.

Figure 279. Large salad bowl in Schleiger no. 266B on Marseille blank no. 9. Haviland & Company, 1888-1896, Marks H and c. $225-275.

Figure 280. Salad bowl in Schleiger no. 266, Diana shape, blank no. 10. Haviland & Company, 1888-1896, Marks H and c. $125-150.

Figure 281. Round salad bowl, 9", in Schleiger no. 275A. Haviland & Company, 1894-1931, Marks I and c. $125-150.

Figure 282. Large footed salad bowl on 12" charger in Schleiger no. 1003. Haviland & Company, 1894-1931, Marks I and c. Bowl $125-175, Charger $95-125.

The Tenth Course: Desserts

Several desserts would be served, all of them rich in cream, sugar and eggs. Sweet pastries, puddings, creams, charlottes and cakes were brought to the table served in fancy Haviland pudding bowls, comports and platters. Each pudding bowl had a porcelain liner with an unglazed bottom. The pudding was poured into the liner, then placed in water and baked slowly at a low temperature until done. The liner was then carried in a towel to the pudding dish, lowered carefully into the dish and then the towel would be gently pulled out from one side. Baked macaroni dishes had no liner but were handled in much the same manner.

Figure 283. Pudding nappie in Schleiger no. 148B. Shown in the 1905 Theodore Haviland Catalog, Mark p. $75-125.

Figure 284. Pudding set with liner in Ranson with hand painted gold trim. Pudding sets usually came with an underplate. Haviland & Company, 1894-1931, Mark I. $225-300.

Figure 285. Pudding set with liner and underplate on Marseille blank. Haviland & Company, 1888-1896, Mark H. *Courtesy of Marty Tackitt.* $325-425.

Figure 286. Pudding set with liner in Schleiger no. 87K on blank no. 22. Haviland & Company, 1894-1931, Marks I and c. *Courtesy of Marty Tackitt.* $250-325.

The Eleventh Course: Ice Cream and Gelatins

Ice cream, and ices made from fruit, were always an important part of every meal. These had to be made in a hand-cranked container and were softer than our ice cream today. The ice cream was then ladled with a large spoon into an ice cream platter, which is deeper than a normal platter. The dessert was then brought to the table, and small matching dishes were filled with the ice cream.

Gelatin molds of every shape and flavor were also served. In the 1800s, gelatin was sometimes called jelly; old cookery books mention ribbon jelly, orange jelly and jelly in molds. There can be some confusion with this term as regular *jelly* was also served during a meal. Both ice cream and gelatin were on the lighter side after such a heavy repast.

Figure 287. Ice Cream Platter by Dammouse. Haviland & Company, 1888-1896, Marks H and c. *Courtesy of Marty Tackitt.* $300-400.

Figure 288. Ice Cream plate and matching dessert plate by Dammouse. Haviland & Company, 1888-1896, Marks H and c. *Courtesy of Marty Tackitt.* Ice cream plate: $95-125. Dessert plate: $75-95.

Figure 290. Ice cream dish in a variation of Schleiger no. 1135. Haviland & Company, 1894-1931, Marks I and c. $65-75.

Figure 289. Old Blackberry ice cream platter 16" in length and 2" in depth, Schleiger no. 1154E. Haviland & Company, 1876-1889, Marks F and g. $225-325.

Figure 291. Ice cream dish in Celadon. Haviland & Company, 1894-1931, Mark c. $35-45.

The Twelve Course: Fruit, Nuts and Cheese

Fresh and candied fruit were brought to the table on fruit stands or comports, and served on special fruit plates. Nuts would probably have been placed in individual nut cups at each place setting (old Haviland catalogs called them almond cups).

Various types of cheese, such as Stilton, would be brought to the table in cheese containers.

At some dinners, the fruit was used as a centerpiece throughout the meal. However, in an 1872 book entitled *Round the Table*, the author had a different opinion. He wrote, *"At a dinner served à la Russe, the dessert must invariably be spoilt before it is eaten. Delicate fruit, such as grapes, strawberries, etc., cannot stand being exposed to the heat of the dining room and the fumes of soups, fish, entrees, and roast meats, without being materially deteriorated."*

Figure 292. Domed cheese dish in Schleiger no. 266B, rare piece. Haviland & Company, 1894-1931, Marks I and c. *Courtesy of Marty Tackitt.* $250-350.

Figure 293. Large fruit bowl in Schleiger no. 1153. Haviland
& Company, 1894-1931, marks I and c. $125-225.

Figure 294. 7¼" square fruit plate in Schleiger no. 133.
Theodore Haviland, 1895, Marks impressed M and n. $75-95.

Figure 295. Fruit bowl in Schleiger no. 226A. Haviland & Company, 1894-1931, Marks I and c. *Courtesy of Marty Tackitt.* $125-150.

Figure 296. Individual almond (or nut) cup in unidentified pattern on smooth blank with gold trim. Haviland & Company, 1894-1931, Marks I and c. $35-50.

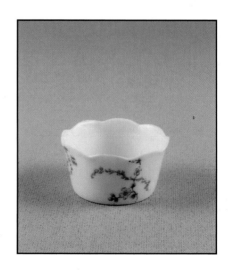

Figure 297. Small nut cup, 2" in diameter, Schleiger no. 394. Very thin porcelain. Charles Field Haviland, 1882-1890, CFH/GDM. $45-55.

The Thirteenth Course:
Coffee and Petit Fours

After-dinner coffee, also called Turkish coffee, was more of an espresso and served in small cups with hot frothed milk. *Petits fours* and bonbons might be brought forth at this time. If this was officially the last course, the ladies would adjourn to the parlor with tea and *petit fours* while the gentlemen stayed in the dining room to drink coffee and brandy and smoke their cigars.

Figure 298. After-dinner coffee cup and saucer in Schleiger no. 842. Theodore Haviland, 1903, Mark p. Much of this pattern seems to have come from S.& G. Gump Co., San Francisco. $40-50.

Figure 299. Turkish coffee cup in Schleiger no. 285. Haviland & Company, 1894-1931, Marks I and c. *Courtesy of Marty Tackitt.* $40-60.

Figure 300. *Petits fours* plate in Torse shape, Schleiger no. 413. Haviland & Company, 1876-1889, Mark F. $150-225.

Figure 301. Small comport in variation of Schleiger no. 442A on blank no. 205 with gold. Haviland & Company, 1894-1931, Marks I and c. *Courtesy of Marty Tackitt.* $165-225.

Figure 302. Bonbon plate with 3 divisions in Marseille, Schleiger no. 9, hand painted. Haviland & Company, 1876-1889, Mark F. $145-225.

Figure 303. Bonbon dish with pierced border, in *Baltimore Rose*, Schleiger no. 1151S. Haviland & Company, 1894-1931, Marks I and c. *Courtesy of Marty Tackitt.* $225-250.

The Fourteenth Course:
Savories

This was an optional course. Those who wanted to impress added it, but most food critics felt this course unnecessary. A savory consisted of a small bite-sized morsel wrapped in pastry. An alternative was a small taste of rich seafood served in a ramekin. Cheese and ham custards were also served in these dishes. The ramekin might also have been used at the *hor d'oerves* or cheese course.

Figure 304. Ramekin cup and saucer in unidentified pattern on blank no. 213 with gold design in center of cup. Haviland & Company, 1894-1931, Marks I and c. $45-55.

Figure 306. Ramekin cup and saucer in Schleiger no. 233, *Norma*. Haviland & Company, 1894-1931, Marks I and c. $45-55.

Figure 305. Ramekin cup and saucer in Schleiger no. 144F. Theodore Haviland, 1903, Mark p. $45-55.

Figure 307. Ramekin cup and saucer in unidentified pattern on blank no. 24 with gold design. Haviland & Company, 1894-1931, Marks I and c. $45-55.

The Fifteenth Course: A Fresh Relay of Finger Bowls, Water and Napkins.

One 1885 cookery book lists this as a course, but most people would only consider food as a course. Professor Eugene La Fayette in his *Family Cook Book* also mentioned a cheese course: an omelette or macaroni garnished with cheese.

Figure 308. This was possibly used as a finger bowl, 2 1/8" high x 4 3/8" diameter. A slightly larger bowl shown in old catalogs is listed as 4 3/4" and was probably used as a waste bowl. In Silver, Schleiger no. 19. Haviland & Company, 1894-1931, Marks I and c. $45-65.

Accessory Pieces for the Table

Mayonnaise Dishes

Mayonnaise was a relatively new dish in the mid-1800s and was frequently placed on the table. Any salad dressing made with raw or hard-boiled eggs was considered mayonnaise. Each pattern of china would have had its own special mayonnaise dish, either a two-piece or one-piece with attached tray. Most dishes are 5" in diameter.

Figure 309. Two-piece mayonnaise dish in leaf shape with gold trim. Haviland & Company, 1894-1931, Mark I and c. $150-175.

Figure 310. Round mayonnaise dish with attached underplate in Schleiger no. 267D. Haviland & Company, 1894-1931, Marks I and c. $125-150.

Mustard Pots

Mustard was served in small containers patterned after full-sized soup tureens. They were 3" to 4" in size, with an opening in the lid for a small silver mustard spoon. Some people have mistaken them for salesmen's samples or doll's china; however, no record has been found, to this date, documenting any doll's china ever made by Haviland. Unfortunately, many of the archives no longer exist; therefore, we can never say never.

A salesman's sample would have special numbers on the bottom indicating tariff prices and sizes, and was usually full size.

Figure 312. Mustard pot in Schleiger no. 320. Theodore Haviland, 1903, Mark p. $150-225.

Figure 311. Mustard pot in Schleiger no. 223. Haviland & Company, 1894-1931, Marks I and c. $150-225.

Figure 313. Mustard pot, hand painted on Marseille blank. Haviland & Company, 1876-1889, Mark F. $150-225.

Salt Cellars

Salt was a prized commodity and served in small salt cellars. Individual salt cellars were placed at every place setting; however, at very large parties or with a shortage of salt cellars, they were placed between guests to share. Salts were usually sold in sets of 12. In the 1927 Catalog of Shapes, they were listed as Celery Salts.

At informal dinners, where guests might pass condiments and small dishes around, one or two master salts were provided. Small silver spoons for each size salt were used.

Butter Dishes

Butter was home churned, kept in tubs and stored in cooling houses or ice boxes. It was made into a mold and served in a three-piece butter dish. A liner or drain was placed inside the dish to keep the butter dry. As the butter warmed up, any milk residue would drip through the holes into the underplate.

The small butter tub might have been used at a tea for small amounts of butter. The butter basket has an opening on the side to pour chilled water into to keep the butter pats firm.

Soft butter was pressed into pretty molds and placed on individual butter dishes. These dishes have also been called *butter pats or butter chips*; but correctly speaking, according to Webster's International Dictionary or the Oxford English, the chip refers to the dish and the pat refers to the butter as well as the wood mold that shapes the butter. Haviland refers to them as individual butter dishes in their catalogs.

Figure 314. Master salt cellar in Schleiger no. 266B. Haviland & Company, 1888-1896, Marks H and c. *Courtesy of Marty Tackitt.* $125-150.

Figure 315. Individual salt cellar in Schleiger no. 91G. Haviland & Company, 1894-1931, Marks I and g. $55-70.

Figure 316. Three-piece butter dish in Schleiger no. 1166 on Ranson blank, twig style. Displayed to show liner, placed inside to keep butter dry. Haviland & Company, 1894-1931, Marks I and c. $125-145.

Figure 319. Butter basket on Osier blank with Meadow Visitor variation. Haviland & Company, 1876-1889, Marks D and g. *Courtesy of Marty Tackitt.* $250-325.

Figure 317. Three-piece butter dish in Schleiger no. 81A on Marseille square blank. Liner is also square. Haviland & Company, 1888-1896, Marks H and c. $125-165.

Figure 320. *Left,* individual butter dish in Schleiger no. 464B, Haviland & Company, 1888-1896, Marks H and i. *Right,* individual butter dish in Schleiger no. 455A, 1894-1931, Marks I and c. $15-25 each.

Figure 318. Butter tub with underplate in Schleiger no. 145, perhaps used to serve several butter pats for a small tea. Theodore Haviland, 1903, Mark p. $95-125.

Figure 321. *Left*, individual butter dish in Schleiger no. 320D. *Right,* individual butter dish in Schleiger no. 162H. Both Theodore Haviland, 1903, Mark p. $15-25 each.

Beverage Containers

Punch, Lemonade and Wine

Punch was usually served at buffets, parties or receptions. Haviland made some exquisite, large punch bowls with underplates, matching punch cups and mugs. Because of the size and fragility, few of the bowls and trays have survived.

Freshly squeezed lemonade was a popular beverage on a hot summer afternoon, served at luncheon, tea time or just for a refreshing break on the veranda.

The wine decanter is a rare piece. As most people used leaded crystal, Haviland did not make very many decanters. This is the only blank found to be used this way.

Figure 322. Punch cup in Schleiger no. 311, from set of twelve. Would have matching punch bowl and possibly underplate. Theodore Haviland, 1903, Mark q. Each $75-95.

Figure 323. Punch set on *Ranson* blank, Schleiger no. 1. Bowl is 7½" high with diameter of 17½". Haviland & Company, 1894-1931, Mark I. *Courtesy of HCIF, Art Wendt Photographer.* $2000-3000.

Figure 324. Drinking mug, one of a set, hand painted in apple pattern, dated 1901. Haviland & Company, 1876-1879, Mark C. *Courtesy of Marty Tackitt.* Each $75-125.

Figure 325. 8½" tall lemonade pitcher in variation of Schleiger no. 70 in green, on Ranson blank. Haviland & Company, 1894-1931, Marks I and c. $225-275.

Figure 326. Tall wine decanter, 12" high, in *Baltimore Rose*, Schleiger no. 1151D. Diameter of neck is only 2". Haviland & Company, 1894-1931, Marks I and c. *Courtesy of R & J Mairs.* $475-675.

Chocolate Pots

Victorian mothers favored chocolate or cocoa as a breakfast and mid-morning beverage for their children, because it was thought to be more nourishing. It was also used as a substitute for tea during the afternoon. Because of the high duty on chocolate, it was an expensive drink usually reserved for the wealthy. It came in bars and was scraped into a pot of hot milk and water until melted, then poured into a Haviland chocolate pot. The pouring spout was at the top of the rim to allow a long-handled silver spoon (a muddler) into the opening to stir the chocolate and keep it from settling on the bottom.

Chocolate sets came with six or eight tall chocolate cups, a creamer and sugar (the chocolate was strong and not presweetened), and possibly a tray on which to display the set. Most of the trays have not survived because they were so thin, without the reinforcement that platters had, and were not meant for carrying, only display. The pots came in various sizes and shapes, and in patterns to match the various Haviland patterns.

Figure 328. Small chocolate pot in Schleiger no. 241H on blank no. 643. Haviland & Company, 1894-1931, Marks I and c. $195-250.

Figure 327. Chocolate pot in Schleiger no. 52D, Ranson blank with gold trim no. 23. Haviland & Company, 1894-1931, Marks I and c. $225-325.

Figure 329. Small chocolate pot in Schleiger no. 346. Theodore Haviland, 1903, Mark p. $195-225.

Figure 330. Small chocolate pot, variation of Schleiger no. 1131 on blank no. 898. Haviland & Company, 1894-1931, Marks I and c. $195-225.

Figure 331. Chocolate set in *Valmont*, Schleiger no. 540 on smooth blank. Haviland & Company, 1911-1931, Marks I and c. Set as shown $400-450.

Figure 332. Chocolate set in Schleiger no. 39D on blank no. 22. Haviland & Company, 1894-1931, Marks I and c. Set as shown $500-650.

Coffee Pots

Coffee was introduced into England in 1653, and into America by 1660. Most coffee was served with hot milk to lighten the taste as it was made very strong; French coffee was made by adding a pint of pre-made coffee to a pint of boiling milk and boiling them together for a short while. Coffee was poured more freely for breakfast and generally served in large cups, while small cups were used for after dinner.

Haviland made coffee pots in several sizes, from individual pots that held two cups to larger pots which held four, six, or eight cups. The catalog of 1889 shows several different tea and coffee sets: Solitaire (for one); Téte-a-téte (for two — "face to face"); and Breakfast or Luncheon (four to six); these came on a tray or stand with cups and saucers, creamer and sugar plus coffee or tea pot. It is very rare to find a complete set today.

Figure 333. Full sized coffee pot in triangular shape, rope handle. Haviland & Company, 1876-1889, English import mark impressed in bottom plus Marks F and g. $225-275.

Figure 334. Individual coffee or tea pot, with demitasse creamer and sugar bowl in variation of Schleiger no. 670 on blank no. 23. Haviland & Company, 1876-1889, Marks F and c. *Courtesy of R & J Mairs.* Set $250-350.

Figure 335. Individual French coffee pot, with side handle in unidentified pattern on smooth blank. Haviland & Company, 1894-1931, Marks I and c. *Courtesy of Marty Tackitt.* $225-275.

Figure 337. *Ganga* coffee pot in Pilgrim shape. Theodore Haviland, 1920-1936, Marks O and r. $195-225.

Figure 336. Eight-cup coffee pot, creamer and sugar bowl in Schleiger no. 42 on blank no. 6. Haviland & Company, 1894-1931, Marks I and c. $325-450.

Tea Pots

Tea was introduced into England in 1666 and became the universal beverage of the British Isles, but was considered a woman's beverage in America. It was served for breakfast and several times during the day, especially for *afternoon tea*, and was generally felt to be more wholesome and less druglike when taken with large quantities of bread and butter, or toast and boiled eggs.

Haviland made tea pots and tea sets in many diverse patterns, from elaborate and expensive to the simple and affordable. Tea cups were made in several different sizes to fit the time of day; four o'clock cups for a small taste, five o'clock cups for an afternoon tea, and regular breakfast or after-dinner tea cups.

The use of silver tea services was most likely preferred by people with money, which may account for the fact that we find so many dinner sets of Haviland china without pots. Coffee or tea pots did not come with sets, but were purchased separately.

Figure 338. Two-cup tea pot with red and gold trim. Charles Field Haviland, CFH/GDA, after 1900. $125-175.

Figure 339. Four-cup tea pot, tea cup and saucer in Schleiger no. 432 on smooth blank with gold trim, sometimes called *Arbor*. Haviland & Company, 1894-1931, Marks I and c. *Courtesy of Marty Tackitt.* Tea pot: $195-225. Tea cup/saucer: $40-45.

160

Figure 340. Four-cup tea pot, creamer and sugar bowl in *Troy*, Schleiger no. 170. Theodore Haviland, 1903, Mark p. Set: $250-350.

Figure 341. Large tea pot on Marseille blank in variation of Schleiger no. 685. Haviland & Company, 1888-1896, Marks H and c. $225-325.

Figure 342. Full-sized tea pot in Schleiger no. 261. Haviland & Company, 1894-1931, Marks I and c. *Courtesy of R & J Mairs.* $225-325.

Cream Pitchers and Sugar Bowls

Haviland breakfast or dinner sets usually came with a matching cream pitcher and sugar bowl. Sets ranged from the individual size to the very large. A porcelain creamer and sugar might be used with a matching Haviland pot or a silver pot; except for very formal occasions, when the majority of serving pieces were silver.

Occasionally an antique store will have the large one-pound sugar bowl mislabeled as a biscuit or cracker jar. The difference, however, is that the sugar bowl has handles.

At a small tea party or a family meal, the milk and sugar was added before the coffee or tea was poured into the cup. At a larger function, the cream and sugar were passed for guests to help themselves. The fancier sets came with open sugar bowls.

Figure 343. Individual creamer and open sugar bowl in *Baltimore Rose* on blank no. 15. Haviland & Company, 1894-1931, Marks I and c. *Courtesy of Marty Tackitt.* $225-275.

Figure 344. Individual creamer and open sugar bowl in Schleiger no. 731. These were most likely part of a Solitaire tea set; tea cup, creamer and sugar bowl, all together on a small tray, to be balanced on a knee. Haviland & Company, 1894-1931, Marks I and c. Complete set $150-250.

Figure 345. Dessert creamer and open sugar bowl in unidentified pattern on blank no. 216. Haviland & Company, 1894-1931, Marks I and c. $150-225.

Figure 346. Demitasse creamer in Schleiger no. 86A. Haviland & Company, 1876-1889, Marks F and c. $60-75.

Figure 347. Demitasse creamer in *Flowering Fields* pattern, Schleiger no. 1157 on smooth blank. Haviland & Company, 1894-1931, Marks I and c. $45-60.

Figure 348. Demitasse cream pitcher in unusual blank and unidentified pattern. Theodore Haviland, 1895-1897, Marks combination of n and o. *Courtesy of R & J Mairs.* $45-65.

Figure 349. Creamer in Schleiger no. 159A. Theodore Haviland, 1903, Mark p. $45-60.

Figure 350. Open sugar bowl and creamer in Schleiger no. 261E. Haviland & Company, 1894-1931, Marks I and c plus Clark Sawyer Company in circle. *Courtesy of R & J Mairs.* $125-145.

Figure 351. Creamer and sugar bowl in Schleiger no. 656A. Haviland & Company, 1894-1931, Marks I and c. $95-125.

Figure 352. Creamer and sugar bowl in Schleiger no. 291A. Haviland & Company, 1894-1931, Marks I and c. $95-125.

Figure 353. Creamer and sugar bowl on Ranson, Schleiger no. 1. Haviland & Company, 1894-1931, Mark I. $95-125.

Figure 354. One-pound sugar bowl and tall stately creamer on *Vermicelli* blank, Schleiger no. 639. Haviland & Company, 1876-1889, Marks F and g. $175-225.

Cups and Saucers

Cups and saucers were made for every circumstance, in every blank and pattern. The older style saucers did not always have a circle for the cup to rest in and are frequently mistaken for sauce dishes, but the sauce dish is deeper than the tea saucer. Shown here are some examples of styles, sizes and unusual cups. One novel item is the mustache cup that allowed the man to drink his morning coffee without getting his mustache wet.

Decorative cups and saucers were frequently part of an elaborate tea or dessert set. Cups and saucers were sometimes made just for commemorative purposes and not part of any set. These usually had the event written on the bottom of the cup with the backstamp, and might have been given as gifts or sold at special exhibitions.

Figure 355. Café au Lait cup and saucer, shading from rust to tan, in Marseille shape. Haviland & Company, 1876-1889, Marks F and c. *Courtesy of Marty Tackitt.* $75-150.

Figure 356. Mustache cup and saucer in *Norma* pattern, Schleiger no. 233. A man could drink from this cup and keep his mustache dry. Haviland & Company, 1894-1931, Marks I and c. *Courtesy of Marty Tackitt.* $125-175.

167

Figure 357. Tall chocolate cup and saucer in Schleiger no. 30B, *Bretagne*. Haviland & Company, 1894-1931, Marks I and c. $40-50.

Figure 358. Tea cup and saucer in Schleiger no. 54, Saxon on Claws blank no. 7. Haviland & Company, 1876-1889, Marks F and c. *Courtesy of R & J Mairs.* $60-75.

Figure 359. Unusual factory decorated tea cup and saucer in smooth blank on pedestal. Haviland & Company, 1894-1931, Marks I and c. $75-125.

Figure 360. Three sizes of cups in Schleiger no. 98, commonly called *Cloverleaf*. From *left*; breakfast coffee cup/saucer, tea cup/saucer, five o'clock cup/saucer. This last cup can also be used on a sandwich tray. Haviland & Company, 1894-1931, Marks I and c. Coffee: $55-65. Tea: $45-50. Five o'clock: $55-65.

Figure 361. Turkish coffee cup 2" high in unidentified pattern. Haviland & Company, 1894-1931, Marks I and c. *Courtesy of Marty Tackitt.* $65-75.

Figure 362. After-dinner coffee cup, saucer and dessert plate in unusual yellow and gold design. Plate is on blank no. 208 with cutouts. Haviland & Company, 1888-1896, Marks H and c. *Courtesy of Marty Tackitt.* Cup/saucer: $65-95. Plate $95-150.

Figure 363. After-dinner coffee cup and saucer in unusual blank. Egyptian symbols are pressed into blank and porcelain is very thin. Haviland & Company, 1876-1879, Marks C and g. $65-85.

Figure 364. After-dinner coffee cup and saucer with butterfly handle, hand painted. Charles Field Haviland, 1875-1882, Mark CFH. $75-125.

Figure 365. Tea cup and saucer from Louisiana Purchase Exhibition held in St. Louis, Missouri, 1904. Theodore Haviland, Mark p plus name and date of exhibition. *Courtesy of Marty Tackitt.* $75-125.

Place Setting Pieces and Identification

The Basic Set

A basic service for 12, as listed in the 1908 Sears catalog, contained dinner plates 9½", tea plates 7½" (called salad plates today), coupe soup plates 7½", 5" sauce/fruit dishes, tea cups and saucers, individual butter dishes 3", plus 12" and 16" meat platters, open oval vegetable dish, covered oval vegetable dish, sauce boat and stand, covered butter dish, 9" pickle dish, sugar bowl and cream pitcher.

Many of the sets purchased at the turn of the century were considered breakfast or luncheon sets, with the largest plate being 8½". These sets were used for tea as well. Perhaps that is why today so many people are searching for dinner plates to complete their service.

In addition to the pieces that have been shown in this book, catalogs of the past list the following pieces available: 5" bun plate; 6 platters ranging in size from 10" to 22"; round chop platters from 12" to 14"; two-piece sauce boat; 3 sizes of salad bowls; 5½" and 6½" berry/ice cream bowls; salad or berry sets, consisting of 8½" bowl and 6 5" bowls; individual service set with 8" plate, oatmeal bowl, individual cream pitcher, cup and saucer; spooner; spoon holder; spoon boat; 5" tumbler plates; powdered sugar; turbot dish; strawberry bowl; asparagus dish and drainer; jelly dish; sardine tray; violet holder; bouquet and knife holder; menu; coffee filter set; macaroni dish on stand (underplate); 14" round fish dish with drainer; toothpick holder; bakers from 7" to 12", and more.

There was a full range of sizes for all plates, pots, pitchers, bowls, etc. Some of the pieces listed above are very rare, and some may have had dual usage as eating habits evolved. As research materials are uncovered in the future, we can be sure to find even more interesting items that were used to enhance the pleasure of dining.

Hand Painted China

China painting was very popular in the late 1880s and early 1900s, and much of the whiteware was used for that purpose. W.A. Maurer, of Council Bluffs, Iowa and Burley & Company, Chicago, Illinois, were two of the companies that published catalogs of white china for decorating, with a large portion containing Haviland pieces. Women of means occupied a portion of their time painting entire sets for the female members of their families.

Figure 366. Dinner plate and tea cup/saucer on blank no. 205. Haviland & Company, 1894-1931, Mark I. Plate $25-35, cup/saucer $35-45.

When Haviland decorated the china at the factory, they placed an additional backstamp along with the whiteware stamp. The whiteware backstamp is slightly blurred because it is under the final glaze, whereas the decorative mark is crisp, darker and placed on top of the glaze. If there is only one backstamp on a decorated Haviland & Company piece, it is probably hand painted. Theodore Haviland frequently used only one backstamp, but sometimes an impression of TH can be found. Haviland whiteware is still popular today and collectible for those who like pure white china.

Figure 367. Luncheon plate and tea cup/saucer on blank no. 10, originally called *Diana*. Haviland & Company, 1888-1896, Mark H. Plate $22-28, Cup/saucer $35-45.

Locating a Pattern

Mrs. Arlene Schleiger published her first book, *Two Hundred Patterns of Haviland China-Book I* in 1950. Before this time, as the majority of them do not have names, there was no way to identify most of the Haviland patterns. Mrs. Schleiger started collecting tea saucers in various patterns and her son, Richard, a student at the College of Architecture in Nebraska, began drawing the patterns. Once the drawings were done, Mrs. Schleiger assigned a number to each pattern. With every variation she found of that pattern, a letter was attached to the number, such as Schleiger #29 (pink roses on Ranson blank no.1), #29A (pink but on smooth blank) and #29M (blue roses on Ranson blank no.1). It is important to know which variation you have to find the correct pattern.

There are now books one through six of *Two Hundred Patterns of Haviland China.* Arlene Schleiger died in 1983, but her son and daughter-in-law Dona have continued the work. As this book goes to press, book number seven is probably complete. The books detail in black-and-white drawings many of the patterns created by the Haviland companies; and as there were over 60,500 different patterns and variations designed, only a portion of the patterns have been sketched and classified. With just a small percentage of the patterns ever named, the Schleiger books have become invaluable in locating patterns.

Several variations of Haviland patterns were done with a change of color, blank, or gold trim. This change could give a completely different look to a pattern and was cost effective as the company did not have to completely reinvent a new pattern.

Haviland collectors and dealers are finding through a study of the backmarks and companies listed on the backs of the pieces that patterns were regional: East Coast tastes varied from West Coast, and certain patterns were more popular in certain areas. The reason we see certain East Coast patterns out West is because grandmother moved West and brought her set with her.

The following photographs are examples of patterns, shapes and gold trims. Some patterns must have been more popular than others, with more pieces manufactured, as certain patterns seem to be more plentiful. On today's market, the larger patterns, such as *Baltimore Rose* and *Drop Rose*, are among the more expensive sets. In the case of *Drop Rose*, the deeper the color, the higher the price.

Figure 368. Coupe luncheon plate and tea cup/saucer in Schleiger no. 133. Theodore Haviland, 1894-1903, Marks M and p. Plate $25-35, Cup/saucer $35-45.

Figure 369. Luncheon plate in Schleiger no. 19, commonly called *Silver Anniversary*, but listed in old catalogs simply as *Silver*. Haviland & Company, 1903-1931, Marks I and c. $20-30.

Figure 371. Dinner plate in variation of Schleiger no. 1174. Haviland & Company, 1894-1931, Marks I and c. *Courtesy of R & J Mairs*. $35-45.

Figure 370. Dinner plate in Schleiger no. 113. Haviland & Company, 1894-1931, Marks I and c. $30-40.

Figure 372. Dinner plate in Schleiger no. 66. Haviland & Company, 1894-1931, Marks I and c. $25-35.

Figure 373. Dinner plate in Schleiger no. 71C. Haviland & Company, 1888-1896, Marks H and c. $25-35.

Figure 375. Dinner plate in Schleiger no. 29, Ranson blank no. 1. Haviland & Company, 1894-1931, Marks I and c. $25-35.

Figure 374. Luncheon plate in *The Princess* pattern, Schleiger no. 57C. There are over 26 variations of this pattern that have been identified. Haviland & Company, 1894-1931, Marks I and c. $20-30.

Figure 376. Dinner plate in Schleiger no. 29N. Haviland & Company, 1894-1931, Marks I and c. $25-35.

Figure 377. Luncheon plate in Schleiger no. 270 on blank no. 22. Haviland & Company, 1894-1931, Marks I and c. $20-30.

Figure 378. Luncheon plate in Schleiger no. 453, sometimes referred to as *Violets and Daisies*. This pattern was also used in railroad china. Haviland & Company, 1894-1931, Marks I and c. $20-30.

Figure 379. Luncheon plate in Schleiger no. 340. Theodore Haviland, 1903, Mark p. $30-40.

Figure 380. Coupe salad plate, after-dinner coffee cup and saucer in Schleiger no. 148B. Theodore Haviland, 1903, Mark p. Plate $20-25. Cup/saucer $40-45.

Figure 381. Luncheon plate in Schleiger no. 55, *Drop Rose* pattern in more common color of soft pink or dusty rose. Haviland & Company, 1894-1931, Marks I and c. $45-55.

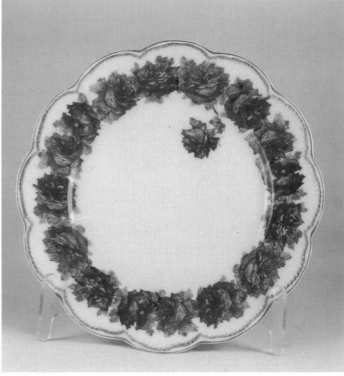

Figure 382. Luncheon plate in Schleiger no. 55, *Drop Rose* pattern in dark pink color. Haviland & Company, 1894-1931, Marks I and c. $65-75.

Jewel Tea Patterns

From the late 1800s until the mid-1960s, the Jewel Tea Company was popular with the homemaker. Like the Fuller Brush man, the Jewel Tea man would go door-to-door selling cleaning products, household products and groceries. In 1911, as a marketing tool, Haviland & Company manufactured a pattern called *The Autumn Leaf*, Schleiger no. 60, which was sold through the Jewel Tea Company. Other variations of this pattern were made, but were not sold by Jewel Tea.

Theodore Haviland created four patterns, Schleiger numbers 149, 150, 151 and 152, which were sold through Jewel Tea in the early 1900s. One early catalog lists the last three patterns as the most expensive china they were selling at that time.

Vallee, a French Limoges Haviland, and an unusual Haviland, *Blue Delph* Coralain, were manufactured and listed for sale in the 1962 Jewel Tea Catalog. *Blue Delph* was advertised as handcrafted in the Caribbean of Coralain, a coral compound designed to withstand heat, staining, scratches, dishwashers — and still look like fine china! Eight place settings without serving pieces sold for $49.95.

Figure 383. Dinner plate, tea cup and saucer in Schleiger no. 60, *Autumn Leaf.* This is the original Jewel Tea pattern that Haviland & Company manufactured. The other variations were not sold by Jewel Tea Company but through china stores. Haviland & Company, 1894-1931, Marks I and c. Plate $25-35, Cup/saucer $40-45.

Figure 384. Round covered casserole and 12" platter in Schleiger no. 60B, a variation of *Autumn Leaf*. Haviland & Company, 1894-1931, Marks I and c. Casserole $95-125, Platter $65-75.

Figure 385. Breakfast coffee cup and saucer in Schleiger no. 60D, a fancy version of *Autumn Leaf* pattern. Haviland & Company, 1894-1931, Marks I and c. $45-65.

Figure 386. Luncheon plate in Schleiger no. 149. Theodore Haviland, 1903, Mark p. $20-30.

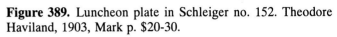

Figure 389. Luncheon plate in Schleiger no. 152. Theodore Haviland, 1903, Mark p. $20-30.

Figure 387. Luncheon plate in Schleiger no. 150. Theodore Haviland, 1903, Mark p. $20-30.

Figure 388. Luncheon plate, tea cup and saucer in Schleiger no. 151. Theodore Haviland, 1903, Mark p. Plate $20-30, Cup/saucer $40-45.

Bird Patterns

The 1920s were called *The Roaring Twenties,* times were fast and styles were changing. Theodore Haviland made several variations of patterns with an oriental look to keep with the decor of the time, and several of the bird patterns were done on the Pilgrim blank.

This is just a sampling of the many bird patterns that were available. Some had just a slight variation with borders and flowers, most had the birds of paradise sitting on a cherry blossom branch and all were vivid in color. By the 1920s, the majority of patterns were given a factory name that was stamped on the back of the china.

Figure 391. Bread and butter plate in unidentified pattern. Same bird and border of *Paradise* or *Chambord*, but without flowers on border. Theodore Haviland, 1925, Mark r. $15-25.

Figure 390. Dinner plate in *Chambord* pattern. Theodore Haviland, 1925, Mark r. $25-35.

Figure 392. Coupe soup bowl in *Eden* pattern. Theodore Haviland, 1925, Mark r. $22-30.

Figure 393. Bread and butter plate in unidentified pattern. Larger plates have two parrots in center. Theodore Haviland, 1925, Mark r. $15-25.

Figure 395. Salad plate in *Rani*. Theodore Haviland, 1925, Mark r. $20-25.

Figure 394. *From left,* salad plates in *Calcutta* and variation, both on Pilgrim blank. Theodore Haviland, 1925, Marks O and r. $20-25.

Figure 396. Small serving bowl with open handles in *Enchantment*, pilgrim blank. Theodore Haviland, 1926, Mark r. $65-75.

Figure 397. Chocolate pot in Schleiger no. 1228. Theodore Haviland, 1925, Mark r. $195-225.

The New Age of Haviland

The Haviland china of today is bolder and brighter, dinner plates are larger and the china has a more substantial feel to it — unlike the Haviland of the late 1800s, which was very light and delicate. Some of the old patterns have been reissued on the new china, but most patterns are of new and modern in design to keep with today's lifestyle.

Collectors plates have been popular over the last 20 years, along with commemorative and decorative ware. Here are just a few samples.

Figure 399. Small round 4" sauce dish in *Vieux Paris* pattern, Haviland & Company, circa 1980. $45-75.

Figure 398. Candlestick in *Margaux*. Haviland & Company, circa 1970-1980. $75-125.

Figure 400. *Malmaison* dinner plate in burgundy. Haviland & Company, 1948-1962, Mark Q. 1980s version is completely different, with blue flowers. $55-75.

Figure 401. Dinner plate, cup and saucer in *Orsay* pattern. Haviland & Company, circa 1968. Plate $30-40, Cup/saucer $40-50.

Figure 402. *Julia,* dinner plate in newer version of Sylvia pattern. Haviland & Company, circa 1980-1990s. $40-60.

Figure 403. Coffee pot in *Sylvia*. Haviland & Company, 1958, Mark s. $225-325.

Figure 404. Large soup tureen in *Vieux Paris* pattern. Haviland & Company, circa 1980s. $350-450.

Figure 405. Daughters of the American Revolution commemorative dish, 4", adapted from the Proscenium, DAR Constitution Hall, signed by Frederick Haviland and dated April 15, 1986. Haviland & Company in the Cannelé blank. $50-75.

Figure 407. Last issue from the Twelve Days of Christmas Series, 1981, *Twelve Drummers Drumming*. Haviland & Company. $65-85.

Figure 406. First issue from Twelve Days of Christmas Series, 1970, *Partridge in a Pear Tree*. Each of the plates portrays one of the Twelve Days. There was a large round platter with all twelve days circling the edge made to accompany the plates. Haviland & Company. $65-85 ea.

Figure 408. *Deck the Boughs* Christmas plate, 1986. This was supposed to be first in series of six, but only one was issued. Haviland & Company. $65-85.

Haviland Blank and Decorator Marks

HAVILAND & CIE. 1842-1931

BLANKS:

Mark A — | HAVILAND DEPOSE | — 1853
Incised on Tablet

Mark B — HAVILAND   H & Co — 1865
Incised

Underglaze Green Marks

Mark C — H & Co — 1876-1879

Mark D — H & Co — 1876-1886

Mark E — H & Co — 1877

Mark F — H & Co / L — 1876-1889

Mark G — H & Co / DEPOSE — 1887

Mark H — H & Co / L / FRANCE — 1888-1896

Mark I — Haviland / France — 1894-1931

DECORATOR MARKS:

Varied Colors Overglaze

Mark a — FABRIQUE PAR HAVILAND & Co POUR J.W. BOTELER & BRO. WASHINGTON   HAVILAND & Co LIMOGES — prior to 1876

Mark b — — 1876-1878

Mark c — HAVILAND & Co Limoges — 1876-1878 / 1889-1931

Mark d — HAVILAND & Co — 1879-1883

Mark e — H & Co ELITE — 1878-1883

Mark f — H & Co SPECIAL — 1879-1889

Mark g — HAVILAND LIMOGES — 1879-1889

Mark h — Haviland & Co Limoges Feu de Four — 1893-1931

Mark i — Décoré par HAVILAND & Co Limoges — 1905-1930 (America) 1926-1931 (France)

HAVILAND & Co. 1875-1885

Haviland Pottery and Stoneware

Mark V — H & Co / L — 1875-1882

Mark W — HAVILAND & Co / Limoges — 1875-1882

Mark X — H & Co / † — 1883-1885

Mark Y — H & Co / L   HAVILAND   HAVILAND LIMOGES — 1883-1885

FRANK HAVILAND 1910-1931

BLANKS:

Mark A1 — *[mark: FRANK HAVILAND LIMOGES]* — 1910-1914

Mark A2 — *[mark: Frank Haviland Limoges]* — 1914-1925

Mark A3 — *[mark: FRANK HAVILAND L B S LIMOGES]* — 1925-1931

THÉODORE HAVILAND 1892-1967

BLANKS:

Colors Usually Green Underglaze

Mark J — *[mark: H monogram]* — 1892

Mark K — *[mark: MONT. MERY ... FRANCE]* — 1892

Mark L — *[mark: Théo Haviland Limoges FRANCE]* — 1893

Mark M — *[mark: T·H]* — 1894-1957

Mark N — *[mark: THEODORE HAVILAND FRANCE]* Blue — 1912

Mark O — *[mark: THEODORE HAVILAND FRANCE oval]* — 1920-1936

Mark P — *[mark: LIMOGES THEODORE HAVILAND shield]* — 1936-1945

Mark Q — *[mark: Haviland France]* — 1946-1962

Mark R — *[mark: Haviland France Limoges]* — 1962

Mark S — *[mark: THEODORE HAVILAND NEW YORK]* Green or Black — 1936

Mark T — *[mark: Theodore Haviland New York MADE IN AMERICA]* Red or Black — 1937-1956

Mark U — *[mark: HAVILAND U. S. A.]* Red — 1957

DECORATOR MARKS:

Colors Green and/or Red Underglaze

Mark j — *[mark: TH circular emblem]* Red — probably 1892

Mark k — *[mark: Porcelaine Mousseline H Limoges FRANCE]* — 1894

Mark l — *[mark: Porcelaine Mousseline T·H Limoges FRANCE]* — 1894

Mark m — *[mark: Porcelaine Theo. Haviland Limoges FRANCE]* — 1895

Mark n — *[mark: Porcelaine Theo. Haviland Limoges FRANCE]* — 1895

Mark o — *[mark: Théodore Haviland Limoges]* — 1897

Mark p — *[mark: Théodore Haviland Limoges FRANCE]* — 1903

Mark q — *[mark: Théodore Haviland Limoges FRANCE]* — 1903

Mark r — *[mark: Théodore Haviland Limoges FRANCE]* — 1925

Mark s — *[mark: HAVILAND LIMOGES FRANCE]* — 1958

Mark t — *[mark: Haviland LIMOGES FRANCE]* — 1967

76

Backmarks are from pages 75 and 76
"Celebrating 150 Years of Haviland China"

Bibliography

Books

Beeton, Isabella. *Beeton's Book of Household Management.* Farrar, Straus and Giroux, 1977.

Chefetz, Sheila. *Antiques for the Table.* New York: Viking Book Company, 1993.

d'Albis, Jean. *Haviland.* Translated by Lauren d'Albis. Paris, France: Dessain et Tolra, 1988.

"The G.C." *Round the Table.* London: Horace Cox, 1872.

Gaston, Mary Frank. *The Collector's Encyclopedia of Limoges Porcelain.* Paducah, Kentucky: Schroeder Publishing Co., Inc., 1980.

Gaston, Mary Frank. *The Collector's Encyclopedia of Limoges Porcelain.* Revised Second Edition. Paducah, Kentucky: Schroeder Publishing Co., Inc., 1994.

Gaston, Mary Frank. *Haviland Collectables & Objects of Art.* Paducah, Kentucky: Schroeder Publishing Co., Inc., 1984.

Jacobson, Gertrude Tatnall. *Haviland China: Volume One.* Des Moines, Iowa: Wallace-Homestead Book Company, 1979.

Jewry, Mary. *Warne's Model Cookery.* London: Frederick Warne and Co., undated.

Klamkin, Marian. *White House China.* New York: Charles Scribner's Sons, 1972.

Klapthor, Margaret Brown. *Official White House China, 1789 to the Present.* Washington, D.C.: Smithsonian Institution Press, 1975.

La Fayette, Prof. Eugene. *Family Cook Book.* London, Chicago and New York: Paris Publishing Co., 1885.

Leventstein, Harvey. *Revolution at the Table: The Transformation of the American Diet.* New York: Oxford University Press, 1988.

McIntyre, Douglas W. *The Official Guide to Railroad Dining Car China.* 20 Cleveland Place, Lockport, New York: Walsworth Press Company, Inc.

Moffit, R. and C. *Old Chinaware Summary, an Aid to Identification.* Muncie, Indiana, 1960.

Paston-Williams, Sara. *The Art of Dining: A History of Cooking and Eating.* London: National Trust, 1993.

Trimble, Alberta C. *Modern Porcelain: Today's Treasures, Tomorrow's Traditions.* New York: Bonanza Books, 1962.

White House Historical Association. *The White House, An Historic Guide.* With the cooperation of the National Geographic Society, Washington, D.C. 1973.

Young, Harriet. *Grandmother's Haviland.* Des Moines, Iowa: Wallace-Homestead Book Company, 1970.

Catalogs and Articles

White China for Decorating, Catalog No. 12. Burley & Company, Chicago, Illinois. Pre-1907.

Haviland Catalog 1879. Haviland and Company.

Grand Prix, Paris, 1889. Haviland and Company.

Animals Modeled by Sandoz, La Porcelaine Theodore Haviland, Limoges, France, 1915-1920. New York: Theodore Haviland & Co.

La Porcelaine Theodore Haviland, Limoges, France. 1905

Catalog of Stoneware and Terra Cotta Pieces. Haviland and Company. No date.

Japonisme: Japanese Influence on French Art 1854-1910. Published jointly by The Cleveland Museum of Art, The Rutgers University Art Gallery and The Walters Art Gallery. No date.

White China Net Price Catalogue No. 45. W.A. Maurer, Council Bluffs Iowa.

An Exception to the Rule, written by Cynthia Adams.

A Catalogue of Our Shapes. Haviland and Company, 1927.

Not to be Taken Lightly, written by Deborah Beaulieu for Victoria Magazines.

Decorative Arts, from a lecture given by John Keefe, Curator of European Decorator Arts at New Orleans Museum, New Orleans, Louisiana, 1993 at the HCIF Conference in San Diego, California.

Theodore Haviland in America, from a lecture given by Annick Moreau, 1993 at the Haviland Collectors Internationale Conference in San Diego, California.

Photo Index

(By Photograph Numbers)